THE ST. GALLEN MAFIA

THE ST. GALLEN MAFIA

Exposing the
Secret Reformist Group
Within the Church

Julia Meloni

TAN Books
Gastonia, North Carolina

Unless otherwise noted, Scripture quotations are from the Douay-Rheims Bible.

Cover design by www.davidferrisdesign.com.

Cover image: The Papal Basilica of Saint Peter in the Vatican, photo by TTstudio/Shutterstock

Library of Congress Control Number: 2021944394

ISBN: 978-1-5051-2287-9
Kindle ISBN: 978-1-5051-2288-6
ePUB ISBN: 978-1-5051-2289-3

Published in the United States by
TAN Books
PO Box 269
Gastonia, NC 28053
www.TANBooks.com

Printed in the United States of America

For my father

"For there is not any thing secret that shall not be made manifest, nor hidden, that shall not be known and come abroad."

—Luke 8:17

Contents

Foreword

For many Catholics, Pope Francis's election was a surprise. This book urges the faithful Catholic to look again. Look into the background, observe the small or dark spaces: great exertions were clearly spent on the 266th pontificate. Only arduous, midnightly labors could have generated (and did generate) the conditions for its possibility.

Back in 2013, Pope Francis's manufactured doctrinal and disciplinary spontaneity seemed to be the hallmark of the new era. And yet Pope Francis's canting forerunners—beginning with Cardinal Martini, who called himself the "ante-pope," one who is not against the pope but who precedes the pope—spent *years* plotting for a like-minded soul to fill the highest position in the Church.

As you are about to read in Ms. Julia Meloni's book, Pope Francis's agenda *is* Cardinal Martini's agenda: the Sankt Gallen agenda. Virtually everything you've been told, or not told, about that agenda was expressed or withheld such as to propagate Pope Francis's views as the "pope of surprises." Yet of all 265 popes since Peter, not a single one of them rivals (or comes anywhere close to rivaling) the degree to which Francis's pontificate was ideologically foreordained.

Needless to say, to a Sankt Gallen mafioso in the know, there wasn't a corpuscle of surprise about what happened at the conclave in March 2013. As shocking as the execution of any mafia conspiracy proves to the rest of the world, its conception and implementation prove to be quite the opposite to its conspirators: ruthlessly exacting discipline, pre-memorized lines and looks, and levels of single-mindedness mixed with unclarity. Or, as Ms. Meloni puts it more aptly: the actuating of the Gallen agenda was a simple matter of "patience" and "time."

So precalculated was the Gallen agenda that, even among outsiders to the mafia, its shock and awe could only be described as partial. The shrewdest opponents of the mafia saw the junta that was coming. Indeed, Cardinal Brandmüller, a *dubia* cardinal and a faithful son of Mother Church, cautioned after only two years of the Francis pontificate, "Communion for the divorced and 'remarried' [comes] first. Then abolition of priestly celibacy, second. Priesthood for women is the ultimate aim, and lastly unification with the Protestants. Then we will have a national German church, independent from Rome. Finally, together with all the Protestants."[1]

As the shadows of his pontificate grow longer, Pope Francis quickens his pace and squares his posture with respect to the unrealized action items on Brandmüller's list (viz., the Gallen list). The execution of the program is the thing! Pope Francis was emplaced to accomplish a short list of goals. This book offers its reader a reasonable basis for firmly believing at least that much. However much damage will be wrought unto the vineyard of the Lord by the time the Gallen agenda is accomplished, at least the reader of this book will see the blows as they come.

The book you prepare to read is, in some sense, a true mafia book. It tells the tale of one *don*—an ante-pope named Cardinal Martini—one underboss called Cardinal Silvestrini, a

---

1   Edward Pentin, *The Rigging of a Vatican Synod: An Investigation into Alleged Manipulation at the Extraordinary Synod on the Family* (San Francisco: Ignatius Press, 2015).

few capos like the man Cardinal Danneels, who revealed the mafia's secrets to the world, and a few handfuls of soldiers. It is the tale of the subversion of the veritable Christian virtues of planning, persistence, and patience. It is the sad narrative of the attempted spoliation of pure things and of a darkling essay into the divinization of wicked things. It also insinuates an unfinished tale of two extant popes: one young conciliar liberal who ripened into a canny, apprehensive, postconciliar conservative who did too much and too little at the end of his pontificate and another young conservative whose fascination with the inscrutable and with political Peronism transformed him, under Cardinal Martini's remote tutelage, into a man following the Gallen mafia's not so hidden agenda.

While the former toils on in darkness and in doubt, the latter approaches the third act of his big performance. He and a small handful of surviving others know how it will end. But to the rest of us, the third act will be marked by surprises, even if uniquely insightful books such as this one have furnished the faithful with key lines and events to await. Alas, even the playbill in hand, like all else in our age, has artfully been rendered inscrutable by the low lights of the theater!

Fast and pray for less strange days. As Pope Benedict XVI once said, would that we might be faithful servants in the vineyard of the Lord! Brothers and sisters, *Deus Vult*! Cross yourselves and march on! Our Lord loves and identifies himself with a suffering servant.

Jesus, Mary, and Joseph, be with us on the Way!

Timothy Gordon, Hattiesburg, Mississippi, USA
May 31, 2021

Acknowledgments

I'm deeply grateful to all the colleagues and readers who have supported this project since its inception.

In a special way, I'd like to thank Patrick O'Hearn and all those at TAN Books who brought this book to publication; Timothy Gordon, who championed this project from a very early stage; Dr. Janet Smith, Dr. Maike Hickson, Matt Gaspers, and Timothy Flanders, who read this book in manuscript form and gave invaluable feedback; and John Vella and John-Henry Westen for editing and publishing my prior articles on the St. Gallen mafia.

I

WAR

1

The Next Pope

Before the 2005 papal election, Cardinal Carlo Maria Martini looked distressed, the papers said.[1] In photos of the Mass before the conclave, you can see him: a tall, glowering old man in red, gripping his cane, staring mutely downward.[2]

"And what does it mean to be children in faith?" asked Cardinal Joseph Ratzinger, the longtime prefect of the Congregation for the Doctrine of the Faith, in the Mass's homily. "St. Paul answers: it means being 'tossed here and there, carried about by every wind of doctrine'" (Eph 4:14).

"How many winds of doctrine have we known in recent decades, how many ideological currents, how many ways of thinking," Ratzinger continued. As he spoke, Martini, the retired archbishop of Milan, looked downward, blinking, as if thinking hard about some insoluble equation. Then he raised

---

1   Daniel Wakin, "A Swift Surge that Defied Expectations," *The New York Times*, April 21, 2005, https://www.nytimes.com/2005/04/21/world/world special2/a-swift-surge-that-defied-expectations.html.

2   See Antonello NUSCA/Gamma-Rapho (Getty Images), *Cardinal Carlo Maria Martini*, April 18, 2005, photograph, https://www.gettyimages .com/detail/news-photo/cardinal-carlo-maria-martini-news-photo/966 212406.

his piercing blue eyes and appeared to glare, for just a moment, at Ratzinger. Then he closed his eyes, fiddled with his cane, and clasped it tightly.[3]

Ratzinger pressed on. He explained how the small boat of Christians had often been wind-tossed, flung by gusts from Marxism to libertinism to syncretism. Then he cried, "Today, having a clear faith based on the Creed of the Church is often labeled as fundamentalism. Whereas relativism, that is, letting oneself be 'tossed here and there, carried about by every wind of doctrine,' seems the only attitude that can cope with modern times. We are building a dictatorship of relativism that does not recognize anything as definitive and whose ultimate goal consists solely of one's own ego and desires."[4]

The dictatorship of relativism. Ratzinger, the son of a German policeman, wanted to warn the cardinals of a danger that he could feel more palpably than others. When he was a boy, one day an eerie new lighthouse sprung up on a hill outside his quiet village—and "at night, when it combed the sky with its glaring light, it appeared to us like a flash of lightning announcing a danger that still had no name," Ratzinger said.[5] Back then, the flash was Nazism; years later, the glint was the dictatorship of relativism and Ratzinger was the sentry in the darkness, warning the post-conciliar Church against an "indiscriminate openness" to an "agnostic and atheistic world."[6]

---

3   "Omelia Santa Messa Pro Pontifice Eligendo 18-04-2005," YouTube video, 18:20, September 27, 2013, https://www.youtube.com/watch?v=vFCi Ak7_Y0Q&t=421s. See 6:50-7:13.

4   "Homily of His Eminence Card. Joseph Ratzinger," Vatican website, April 18, 2005, http://www.vatican.va/gpII/documents/homily-pro-eligendo -pontifice_20050418_en.html.

5   Joseph Ratzinger, *Milestones: Memoirs* (San Francisco: Ignatius Press, 1998), 16, Kindle.

6   Joseph Ratzinger, *The Ratzinger Report: An Exclusive Interview on the State of the Church* (San Francisco: Ignatius Press, 1985), 37.

But now there was something subterranean that was concentrating all its energies on toppling him. Something that had stayed quietly underground for a decade, building pressure and waiting.

* * *

Somewhere in a small, old journal, a photo with an understated caption proves that they met. Entitled "A Visit Enjoyed by Friends," the photograph shows Martini and a group of European cardinals lined up like a football team, say those who have seen it.[7]

There was Cardinal Godfried Danneels, a Belgian known for his discretion, diplomacy, and intelligence. Known, too, for his liberal views on sexuality, Danneels emerged as one of the media's "outsider" candidates for pope.

There was Cardinal Walter Kasper, the smiling German theologian with glasses, dubbed "Kasper the Friendly Cardinal" by the media.[8] He had sparred with Ratzinger for years over the "Kasper proposal" to open up Communion to the divorced and civilly remarried.

There was Cardinal Cormac Murphy-O'Connor, the tall, likable Englishman with a contagious laugh and a quiet sense of revolution. A natural ecumenist, he knew how to make people feel comfortable, and they gravitated toward him.

Then there was Cardinal Achille Silvestrini, the maneuvering, over-eighty Italian diplomat.

Martini, Danneels, Kasper, Murphy-O'Connor, Silvestrini. They were the key members and alumni of the St. Gallen mafia, and just days after Pope John Paul II's funeral, they secretly met at the Villa Nazareth, a Roman college residence, at Silvestrini's

---

7   "Notebook: Every Picture," *The Tablet*, July 23, 2005.
8   Paul Elie, "The Pope in the Attic: Benedict in the Time of Francis," *The Atlantic*, May 2014, www.theatlantic.com/magazine/archive/2014/05/the -pope-in-the-attic/359816/.

invitation.[9] The way German journalist Paul Badde heard it, they had the "absolute aim" of getting Ratzinger "out of the race" so they could elect Martini as pope.[10]

Martini. For over a decade, the world had hoped that Martini, a Jesuit, would make the Church swim with it in the undulating seas of postmodernity. In 1993, the London *Sunday Times Magazine* published Martini's full-color photo with the glowing headline: "The Next Pope?" The accompanying interview—a glossy showpiece of ambiguity and indirection—hinted at movement on everything from contraception to women priests.[11]

The press, clearly fascinated, hailed Martini's "discreet" and "Jesuitical" approach to changing the Church. Would Martini be the "new, cool pope?" asked *The Independent* in 1994. "Churches unite in their taste for Martini," ran another 1994 headline in *The Observer*.

It was the 1990s, John Paul II was quietly suffering from Parkinson's disease, and the timing seemed right for a Martini-led revolution. "If there had been a conclave a decade earlier [than the 2005 conclave], Martini might, I think, have been elected pope," Murphy-O'Connor later said.[12]

And so in 1996, when the revolutionaries held him up as the next pope, Martini founded the St. Gallen mafia. Its glue—according to Danneels's authorized biography—was not an idea but a

9   Edward Pentin, "Still Controversial: Cardinal Danneels and the Conclave of 2005," *The National Catholic Register*, November 5, 2015, https://www.ncregister.com/news/still-controversial-cardinal-danneels-and-the-conclave-of-2005-9bx1q46a.

10   Pentin, "Still Controversial."

11   John Cornwell, "The Next Pope?," *Sunday Times Magazine*, April 25, 1993.

12   Cormac Murphy-O'Connor, *An English Spring: Memoirs* (London: Bloomsbury, 2015), 148, NOOK.

person. The group's spark derived from its opposition to Ratzinger, the right-hand man of John Paul II's conservative papacy.[13]

"The idea was simple: to gather these powerful, like-minded prelates together to use their vast networks of contacts to bring about what political analysts would recognize as 'regime change,'" explains historian Henry Sire. As Sire points out, the mafia shrouded its agenda in harmless-sounding language about "decentralization." "It would be naive not to recognize that the slogans of decentralization and collegiality used by the group were code words for a broad liberal program," says Sire.[14]

It was a program that surrendered to the dictatorship of relativism—and Martini should have been the pope to usher it in. But in the mid-1990s, something began shaking Martini's world.

It started as a quiet tremor of the hand that a colleague noticed when Martini spoke in public. Inexorably, the trembling progressed, until he could no longer deny nor hide it.[15]

Martini had Parkinson's disease.

* * *

"Martini was well aware that after John Paul II's long illness, the Church could not afford to have another ill pope," said Silvestrini after the conclave. "In 2005 the effects of the Parkinson's disease which Martini was suffering from became apparent; hence he could not really present himself as a candidate for the papacy."[16]

---

13   Jürgen Mettepenningen and Karim Schelkens, *Godfried Danneels: Biographie* (Antwerpen: Uitgeverij Polis, 2015), 448, https://pure.uvt.nl/ws/portalfiles/portal/28312169/Danneels_Polis_FR.pdf.

14   Marcantonio Colonna [Henry Sire], *The Dictator Pope: The Inside Story of the Francis Papacy* (Washington, DC: Regenery, 2017), 7, 9, Kindle.

15   Andrea Tornielli, *Carlo Maria Martini: El Profeta del Diálogo* (Santander: Sal Terrae, 2013), loc. 2145 of 2606, Kindle.

16   "Parkinson's Prevented Martini from Entering Conclave as Potential Papal Candidate," *La Stampa*, September 1, 2012, https://www.lastampa.it/vatican-insider/en/2012/09/01/news/parkinson-s-prevented-martini

But at the time of the conclave, "some wanted to believe Martini's health wasn't as poor as he had claimed," says a Vatican expert. "Perhaps Martini's new cane, which no one had seen him using before the pope's funeral, was simply a prop, a silent signal that the others should not think of him as a potential pope."[17]

"Others strategized," the expert continues. "If they could park the anti-Ratzinger votes with Martini, that would buy them some time to rally support around another candidate."[18]

And so Martini gathered his cane and prepared to ready the way for the next pope. "He agreed to be considered as a candidate but only as a 'flag-bearer,' in order to allow his supporters to count how many there were," says another vaticanista.[19]

On the same day that he secretly met at the Villa Nazareth to plot how to stop Ratzinger, Martini spoke first at the pre-conclave meetings of cardinals called General Congregations. There he named the issues that the next pope would have to face in a new way—from collegiality to sexuality.[20]

Then, when his minutes were up and yet no one would speak, Martini stood up.

He said he still had something to say.

-from-entering-conclave-as-potential-papal-candidate-1.36374341.

17   Robert Blair Kaiser, *A Church in Search of Itself: Benedict XVI and the Battle for the Future* (New York: Vintage, 2006), 214, Kindle.

18   Kaiser, *A Church in Search*, 214.

19   Andrea Tornielli, "Martini: Benedict XVI's Resignation and the 2005 Conclave," *La Stampa*, July 18, 2015, https://www.lastampa.it/vatican-in sider/en/2015/07/18/news/martini-benedict-xvi-s-resignation-and-the -2005-conclave-1.35243041. "Vaticanista" is a term used to describe a journalist who covers the Vatican.

20   Luigi Accattoli, "Il Cardinale Martini nel Conclave del 2005," *Luigi Accattoli* (blog), September 1, 2012, http://www.luigiaccattoli.it/blog/articoli-del -corriere-della-sera/il-cardinale-martini-nel-conclave-del-2005/.

In the hushed silence, Martini spoke of his program for the next pope. He spoke of decentralizing the Church. He spoke (as he later said) of the "new answers" that the next pope would "have to give" on sexuality and Communion for the divorced and civilly remarried.[21] According to the papers, he even spoke of a possible diaconate for women.[22]

Meanwhile, Silvestrini—too old to take part in the conclave himself—served as the revolutionaries' "mastermind."[23] Silvestrini had "replaced" Martini in the mafia after the latter revealed his Parkinson's diagnosis in 2002 and retired to Jerusalem.[24] According to an anonymous cardinal from Latin America who knew Silvestrini well, the Italian was a "formidable maneuverer."[25]

With Silvestrini's arrival in 2003, the mafia became increasingly fixated on planning for John Paul II's succession. "When Cardinal Silvestrini joined the group it took on a more tactical and strategic character," confirms a biographer of Danneels.[26]

Silvestrini had been close to John Paul II for decades and, according to Danneels's biography, he fed the mafia firsthand

21 Carlo Maria Martini and Georg Sporschill, *Night Conversations with Cardinal Martini*, trans. Lorna Henry (New York: Paulist Press, 2012), 33, NOOK.

22 Giancarlo Pani, "Women and the Diaconate," *La Civiltà Cattolica*, April 12, 2017, https://www.laciviltacattolica.com/women-and-the-diaconate/.

23 Evangelina Himitian, *Francisco: El Papa de la Gente* (Aguilar, 2013), loc. 2835 of 3931, Kindle.

24 Mettepenningen and Schelkens, *Godfried Danneels*, 456.

25 Nicolas Diat, *L'Homme Qui Ne Voulait Pas Être Pape: Histoire Secrète d'un Règne* (Paris: Albin Michel, 2014), 97.

26 Jeanne Smits, "Cardinal Danneels Admits Being Part of Clerical 'Mafia' that Plotted Francis's Election," LifeSiteNews, September 25, 2015, https://www.lifesitenews.com/news/cardinal-danneels-admits-being-part-of-clerical-mafia-that-plotted-francis.

information about the pontiff's declining health.[27] When John Paul II died on April 2, 2005, Silvestrini was one of the last people to see him.

"He gave us a look of recognition," Silvestrini told reporters. "I kissed his hand. I caressed his brow, and I said, 'Thank you, Holy Father, for all you have done for the church.' He seemed to have understood."[28] Then, just three days after John Paul II's funeral, Silvestrini invited Martini and the mafia to the Villa Nazareth for their anti-Ratzinger plotting session.

One day, the mafia sent off signals of Silvestrini's plan. Sitting with a gin and tonic, Murphy-O'Connor gave his then press secretary, Austen Ivereigh, "little steers" about candidates.

Murphy-O'Connor asked, "What do you know about the Latin Americans?"

Cutting Ivereigh off, he said, "What about [the cardinal from] Buenos Aires?"[29]

* * *

Jorge Mario Bergoglio. The St. Gallen mafia had watched the shy Jesuit from Buenos Aires for some time.

A man of many nicknames, Bergoglio was a riddle, an enigma. To some who had been drawn into his orbit during his "ultraconservative" days, the Jesuit was known simply as *El*,

27   Mettepenningen and Schelkens, *Godfried Danneels*, 456.

28   Elaine Sciolino and Daniel Wakin, "Pope's Visitors Saw Serenity in Final Hours," *The New York Times*, April 4, 2005, https://www.nytimes.com/2005/04/04/world/europe/popes-visitors-saw-serenity-in-final-hours.html.

29   Austen Ivereigh, "Cormac the Kingmaker: The Lesson that Proved Decisive in the Election of Pope Francis," *The Tablet*, September 6, 2017, https://www.thetablet.co.uk/news/7714/cormac-the-kingmaker-the-lesson-that-proved-decisive-in-the-election-of-pope-francis.

"like God."[30] To others, Bergoglio was *La Gioconda*, the inscrutable "Mona Lisa."[31]

To some, he was *Carucha*—"Long Face"—because of "the pious long faces which he puts on when he takes Communion or when you meet him in the corridors with his head tilted to one side."[32] To others, that was all a "façade," and Bergoglio was a "methodical" Jesuit "commando" inside.[33]

But to more than one cardinal in St. Gallen, he was the next pope.

In February 2001, Bergoglio, known as a conservative, became a cardinal. So did three mafia members: Kasper, Murphy-O'Connor, and Karl Lehmann. Bergoglio became especially good friends with Murphy-O'Connor, and they sat together at events in a group nicknamed *La Squadra*.[34]

According to Ivereigh, Bergoglio then used his time in Rome later that year to reconnect with Martini, whom he had known since at least the mid-1970s. Ivereigh says that Martini, whom Bergoglio liked to quote, then introduced the Latin American to the mafia—"initiating relationships that would develop on Bergoglio's fleeting visits to Rome in the next years."[35]

In this way, says Sire, Bergoglio signaled to the mafia that he was an ally, a fellow traveler, despite his longtime conservative reputation.[36]

It worked like a charm.

---

30   Paul Vallely, *Pope Francis: The Struggle for the Soul of Catholicism* (London: Bloomsbury, 2015), loc. 1358 of 11236, Kindle.

31   Elisabetta Piqué, *Pope Francis: Life and Revolution: A Biography of Jorge Bergoglio* (Chicago: Loyola Press, 2014), 73, Kindle.

32   Austen Ivereigh, *The Great Reformer: Francis and the Making of a Radical Pope* (New York: Henry Holt & Co., 2014), 78, 67, Kindle.

33   Francesca Ambrogetti and Sergio Rubin, *Pope Francis: His Life in His Own Words* (New York: G.P. Putnam's Sons, 2010), 52, Kindle.

34   Murphy-O'Connor, *An English Spring*, 151.

35   Ivereigh, *The Great Reformer*, 262–263.

36   Sire, *The Dictator Pope*, 39.

tion.8

Martini.

At its January 2002 meeting, the Gallen group made Bergoglio's performance at a 2001 synod a topic of conversation. Multiple mafia members admired the Latin American due to his interest in decentralization.[37]

Eventually, according to author Nicolas Diat, Silvestrini tried to convince Bergoglio to lead the anti-Ratzingerian contingent. But ironically—according to a Latin American cardinal who knew Silvestrini well—Silvestrini's "big problem" came from Martini.[38]

Martini "absolutely" refused to back Bergoglio, his fellow Jesuit. Martini had been close to the longtime general of the Jesuits, Pedro Arrupe, who presided over the order's liberalization and politicization in the 1970s. Bergoglio, however, took issue with various aspects of Arrupe's radical line. Ultimately, despite repeated efforts, Silvestrini could not surmount this tension between Martini and Bergoglio.[39]

And yet there was something about Bergoglio—some quiet, mysterious spark—that kept the others drawn in. On the eve of the conclave, in Silvestrini's Vatican apartment, various mafia members and allies converged on Bergoglio's candidacy.

"The cardinals linked to the Sankt Gallen group and others too concluded that Bergoglio was the candidate best suited to be the next pope," says a vaticanista. "They believed that, in a pastoral sense, he represented a change from the previous pontificate, and so they decided to support him in the election."[40]

* * *

On April 18, 2005, Martini gathered his cane and proceeded

---

37 Mettepenningen and Schelkens, *Godfried Danneels*, 453.
38 Diat, *L'Homme*, 97.
39 Diat, *L'Homme*, 97–98. For a discussion of the politicization of the Jesuits, see Sire, *The Dictator Pope*, 26–27.
40 Gerard O'Connell, *The Election of Pope Francis: An Inside Account of the Conclave that Changed History* (Maryknoll, NY: Orbis, 2019), 44, NOOK.

into the Sistine Chapel to elect the next pope. After taking a solemn oath swearing not to break the conclave's rules nor reveal its secrets, he and the other cardinals heard the thud of the locked door.

Above the altar, Michelangelo's fresco of the Last Judgment loomed, its triumphant Christ in the heavens proclaiming his rulership over history and time.

Below, the cardinals lodged their ballots one by one into a gold urn.

On the first ballot, some forty or more of the 115 cardinals voted for Ratzinger. Some, but not many, voted for Martini; others voted for Bergoglio.[41]

Black smoke funneled out, announcing no pope had been chosen.

As the voting continued, Martini's votes passed to Bergoglio. A "dramatic struggle" between the Gallen group and Ratzinger's supporters took shape.[42] Martini spread the word that Ratzinger was not "apt" to find the requisite consensus—raising hopes that the German might withdraw so a compromise candidate could emerge.[43]

Black smoke rose again outside.

Then, at the end of the third ballot, Ratzinger surpassed fifty-eight votes.

---

41 John Allen Jr., *The Rise of Benedict XVI: The Inside Story of How the Pope Was Elected and Where He Will Take the Church* (New York: Doubleday, 2007), 105, NOOK.

42 Edward Pentin, "Archbishop Gänswein: Benedict XVI Sees Resignation as Expanding Petrine Ministry," *The National Catholic Register*, May 23, 2016, https://www.ncregister.com/blog/archbishop-gaenswein-benedict-xvi-sees-resignation-as-expanding-petrine-ministry.

43 Maike Hickson, "Pope Benedict's Biographer: Leftist Cardinal Tried to Stop Ratzinger's 2005 Papal Election," LifeSiteNews, May 1, 2020, https://www.lifesitenews.com/blogs/pope-benedicts-biographer-leftist-cardinal-tried-to-stop-ratzingers-2005-papal-election.

"Though no one said so out loud," says vaticanista John Allen Jr., "most of the cardinals felt the handwriting was on the wall."[44]

The writing was on the wall because, as vaticanista Marco Politi explains, John Paul II's 1996 text *Universi Dominici Gregis* had upended the familiar procedures for electing popes. In previous conclaves, a candidate could accumulate enough votes to block another from reaching the two-thirds threshold—forcing a third, compromise candidate to emerge. But under the new rules, Ratzinger's supporters just needed to hold out for over thirty-four ballots. Then the requirement for election would change from the two-thirds threshold (seventy-seven votes) to a simple absolute majority (fifty-eight votes).[45]

Politi likens attaining this absolute majority of votes to "putting a sword on the table."[46] According to him and others, some of Ratzinger's supporters indicated that they were prepared to hold out as long as necessary.[47]

But there was a twist.

According to a cardinal who knew Ratzinger, had the conclave dragged on, the German would have asked his supporters to shift their votes to Cardinal Camillo Ruini.[48]

And rumor had it that Martini dreaded a conservative Ruini papacy so much that he preferred to act as the *deus ex machina* for Ratzinger's rise.[49]

---

44   Allen, *The Rise of Benedict XVI*, 107.

45   Marco Politi, *Joseph Ratzinger: Crisi di un Papato* (Rome: Laterza, 2015), 52–53, NOOK. See also Vallely, *Pope Francis*, loc. 607 of 11236.

46   Politi, *Joseph Ratzinger*, 52.

47   Politi, *Joseph Ratzinger*, 52–53; Vallely, *Pope Francis*, loc. 615 of 11236.

48   Diat, *L'Homme*, 83.

49   For this theory, espoused by Alberto Melloni and others, see Sandro Magister, "Vatican Storylines: Those Who Are Resisting Benedict XVI," *L'Espresso*, January 19, 2006, http://chiesa.espresso.repubblica.it/articolo /44944%26eng%3dy.html; and Sandro Magister, "Conclave: Tradition Makes a Comeback," *L'Espresso*, August 7, 2007, http://chiesa.espresso .repubblica.it/articolo/159201%26eng%3Dy.html.

An aura of mystery, thick as the black smoke of the incinerated conclave ballots, enshrouds what happened next. According to vaticanista Bernard Lecomte, multiple eyewitnesses saw a mysterious lunchtime conversation between Martini and Ratzinger before the fourth ballot. The arm-in-arm conversation left at least one witness with the impression that Martini had shunted his votes to Ratzinger, possibly in exchange for a guarantee about the new pontificate's orientations.[50]

Notably, Ratzinger always denied the existence of any kind of electoral "agreement."[51]

But was Martini up to something that did not involve a pact?

Why did Politi,[52] Marco Garzonio,[53] Alberto Melloni,[54] and other respected Vatican experts soon insist that Martini, *in extremis*, had instructed his supporters to back Ratzinger?

Why was it said that, during the same lunch break, Bergoglio had indicated that his own supporters should vote for Ratzinger?[55] After the conclave, back in Argentina, why was the word that Bergoglio had felt "used" by the anti-Ratzinger party?[56]

Why, after lunch, did Ratzinger so swiftly metamorphose into Pope Benedict XVI, one of the fastest popes to be elected in the past hundred years, elevated after just four ballots?[57]

50 Bernard Lecomte, *Secretos del Vaticano* (Buenos Aires: El Ateneo, 2014), 305.

51 Elio Guerriero, *Benedict XVI: His Life and Thought* (San Francisco: Ignatius Press, 2010), 464, footnote 12, Kindle. See also Aldo Maria Valli, *Benedetto XVI: Il Pontificato Interrotto* (Milan: Mondadori, 2013), 30.

52 Politi, *Joseph Ratzinger*, 54.

53 Marco Garzonio, "Perché Martini Avrebbe Apprezzato L'Addio," *Corriere della Sera*, February 13, 2013.

54 Magister, "Conclave: Tradition Makes a Comeback."

55 Ivereigh, *The Great Reformer*, 284.

56 Piqué, *Pope Francis*, 2.

57 Allen, *The Rise of Benedict XVI*, 103.

Why did Murphy-O'Connor tell the media that some of the hold-outs had suddenly decided to switch their votes to Ratzinger for the "unity" of the Church?[58]

When the new pope came out onto St. Peter's loggia, he looked radiant, flush with the glow of having triumphed over some great battle. Badde, the journalist who had leaked details of the mafia's conclave plot against Ratzinger, thought that the new pope looked like a boxer with his arms high over St. Peter's.

"All the weight of the world that seems often to have oppressed and shackled Joseph Cardinal Ratzinger, as recently as yesterday, has suddenly fallen away from him," thought Badde. "Once again he throws his arms high, and again! No one has ever seen him this way, not even himself. Nothing is too big for him, not the crimson stole, not the white skullcap, not even the shoes of his predecessor."[59]

Martini, meanwhile, gathered his cane and prepared to return to Jerusalem.

A few weeks after the conclave, Martini was hospitalized with heart problems. He had to receive a pacemaker.[60] Some speculated that the stress of the conclave was not irrelevant.

Asked once about what had happened in the conclave, Martini said, "Lead me not into temptation."[61]

But when asked what kind of pope Benedict would be, the old cardinal grew effusive.

Expect "beautiful surprises," Martini said.[62]

58   Wakin, "A Swift Surge that Defied Expectations."
59   Paul Badde, *Benedict Up Close: The Inside Story of Eight Dramatic Years* (Irondale, AL: EWTN, 2017), loc. 90 of 3349, Kindle.
60   Kaiser, *A Church in Search*, 217.
61   Kaiser, *A Church in Search*, 217.
62   Marco Garzonio, *Il Profeta: Vita di Carlo Maria Martini* (Milan: Mondadori, 2012), 435.

2

Silvestrini

The night of Pope Benedict's election, a Latin American cardinal ran into Silvestrini on the street close to St. Peter's.

He was a "defeated man," says the cardinal of Silvestrini.

The cardinal saw Silvestrini's "dull anger"—saw his refusal to accept a papal election that marked the very negation of his life's work. He saw Silvestrini's stubborn notion that Ratzinger would only be a transitional pope.

That evening, the cardinal saw that Silvestrini had declared "a form of war."[1]

* * *

A few months after Benedict's election, which he likened to the falling blade of a guillotine, a mysterious conclave diary appeared.

It read, many said, like an early assault on Benedict's pontificate—and a piece of campaign material for Bergoglio's next papal run.

---

1   Nicolas Diat, *L'Homme Qui Ne Voulait Pas Être Pape: Histoire Secrète d'un Règne* (Paris: Albin Michel, 2014), 98.

Claiming to offer hard vote counts from an anonymous cardinal, the diary alleged that on the first ballot, Ratzinger earned
forty-seven votes, Martini earned nine, and Bergoglio earned
ten. The accompanying article noted how auspicious it was that
Bergoglio had beaten Martini by one vote—and disclosed that a
group including Danneels drove Bergoglio's support.[2]

Then the piece gestured toward Bergoglio's pastoral subver-
siveness. It reported how, on the conclave's eve, Bergoglio had
joked to some friends that John Paul II's collaborators on the
topic of sexual ethics wanted "to stick the whole world inside
a condom."[3] It was an acid barb against precisely the kind of
pastoral "rigidity" presumably embodied by Ratzinger.

Eventually, the diary alleges, Bergoglio reached a sufficient
number of votes (forty) to block Ratzinger from reaching the
number needed for election (seventy-seven). But then it became
uncertain whether Bergoglio would even accept the papacy.

As the diarist said of Bergoglio: "I watch him as he goes to
deposit his ballot in the urn on the altar of the Sistine Chapel:
his gaze is fixed upon the image of Jesus, who is judging souls
at the end of time. There is suffering written on his face, as if he
were imploring: 'God, don't do this to me.'"[4]

On the final scrutiny, Bergoglio lost almost fifteen votes.
Ratzinger won the papacy with eighty-four. Bergoglio's humility
before *The Last Judgment* had helped clinch Ratzinger's victory.

But this narrative was, as many soon realized, a revisionist
history, etched by some anti-Ratzingerian hand.

---

2   Lucio Brunelli, "Così Eleggemmo Papa Ratzinger," *Limes*, September
      23, 2005, https://www.limesonline.com/cosi-eleggemmo-papa-ratzinger
      /5959. All further quotations of the diary are from this source.

3   Quoted in Paul Vallely, *Pope Francis: The Struggle for the Soul of Catholi-
      cism* (London: Bloomsbury, 2015), loc. 2542 of 11236, Kindle.

4   Sandro Magister, "The Vatican Codes: This is How I Rewrite My Con-
      clave," *L'Espresso*, October 7, 2005, http://chiesa.espresso.repubblica.it/
      articolo/40137%26eng%3dy.html.

First came the issue of whether the diary's vote counts could be trusted.

Based on conversations with eight different cardinals, vaticanista John Allen Jr. determined that Ratzinger in fact ended up with almost 100 out of 115 votes—not the diary's 84.[5] Likewise, several cardinals, without disclosing exact numbers, told Nicolas Diat that Ratzinger received more votes on the last ballot than the 84 reported by the diarist.[6]

Next came the question of whether Bergoglio really "refused" to become pope if elected.

According to vaticanista John Thavis, while some accept that reading, others insist that Bergoglio never shut down the possibility of becoming pope. They say he simply indicated, mainly in gestures, that he felt humbled by the thought.[7]

Then came the issue of whether Bergoglio, with his alleged forty votes, really could have blocked Ratzinger from becoming pope.

In times past, a candidate with such numbers could indeed trigger a search for a third, compromise candidate. But as vaticanista Marco Politi stresses, John Paul II's revision of conclave rules in 1996 upended that established script. It enabled a candidate with fifty-eight or more votes to be elected if his support held up for over thirty-four rounds. By the end of the third ballot, Ratzinger had already secured the set number of votes.

According to Politi, once Ratzinger secured this majority, Bergoglio's supporters realized that they could not win. As one

5   John Allen Jr., *The Rise of Benedict XVI: The Inside Story of How the Pope Was Elected and Where He Will Take the Church* (New York: Doubleday, 2007), 109, NOOK.

6   Diat, *L'Homme*, 96.

7   John Thavis, "An Argentine Cardinal Who's Quietly Drawing Attention— Again," *John Thavis* (blog), March 10, 2013, https://www.johnthavis.com /post/an-argentine-cardinal-who-s-quietly-drawing-attention-again.

European cardinal put it, they understood that Bergoglio would not get "one more vote."[8]

But that did not stop the revolutionaries from downsizing Ratzinger's victory with the stroke of a pen—making it seem as if he barely met the threshold for becoming pope.

The diary was a brilliant piece of propaganda. Soon, the papers were accepting the diary's vote counts at face value, perpetuating its anti-Ratzingerian narratives.

And according to Diat, a number of high-ranking prelates believe that the cardinal who leaked the mysterious diary was none other than Silvestrini.[9]

* * *

Silvestrini. He didn't make as many headlines as Martini, but the powerful diplomat was locked in a battle with Ratzinger's conservative worldview.

In 1980, while advocating for an anti-abortion referendum, historian Roberto de Mattei saw firsthand why Silvestrini had been called the "spiritual son" of an ultra-progressive.

According to de Mattei, in a "smarmy tone," the then bishop Silvestrini advised against the anti-abortion measure. He accused it of embodying a damaging "counter-catechesis" on abortion. He said that pro-abortionists would become emboldened because of it. Even as de Mattei protested against such defeatist logic, Silvestrini pressed on. Then de Mattei witnessed firsthand the "politics of surrender by the men of the Church."[10]

8   Marco Politi, *Joseph Ratzinger: Crisi di un Papato* (Rome: Laterza, 2015), 54, NOOK.

9   Diat, *L'Homme*, 99–100.

10   Roberto de Mattei, "The Revolt Against *Humanae Vitae* Continues to Haunt Us Today," LifeSiteNews, May 25, 2018, https://www.lifesitenews .com/opinion/the-revolt-against-humanae-vitae-continues-to-haunt-us -today.

For Silvestrini—the plotter, the maneuverer—knew how to make both war and peace.

Silvestrini was a major engineer of *Ostpolitik*—the Vatican policy that, according to de Mattei, "attributed a positive value to modernity, of which Communism appeared to be the ultimate expression. Communism wasn't to be condemned, but purified of its atheism and reconciled with Christianity."[11]

But Communism had its own radical endgame. According to the thinking of a founder of the Italian Communist party, Antonio Gramsci, Communism was to devolve into secularism and relativism. Proteus-like, the "dictatorship of the proletariat" morphed into the "dictatorship of relativism," and Gramsci's plan for societal secularization pressed inexorably forward.[12]

"After the collapse of the Soviet Union, [Communism's] errors were as if released from the wrapping that contained them, to propagate like an ideological miasma over the entire West, under the form of cultural and moral relativism," says de Mattei.[13]

And so it fell to Ratzinger to fight the dictatorship of relativism with the defense of "non-negotiable" principles.

Christians are "called to reject, as injurious to democratic life, a conception of pluralism that reflects moral relativism," said Ratzinger's Congregation for the Doctrine of the Faith in 2002. "Democracy must be based on the true and solid foundation of non-negotiable ethical principles," it continued, insisting on the absolute imperative to defend life and the family.[14]

---

11   Roberto de Mattei, "Fatima 100 Years Later: A Marian Call for the Whole Church," *Rorate Caeli* (blog), October 13, 2017, https://rorate-caeli.blogspot.com/2017/10/de-mattei-fatima-100-years-later-marian.html.

12   Roberto de Mattei, *Love for the Papacy & Filial Resistance to the Pope in the History of the Church* (Brooklyn, NY: Angelico Press, 2019), 171.

13   De Mattei, *Love for the Papacy*, 170.

14   Congregation for the Doctrine of the Faith, "Doctrinal Note on Some Questions Regarding the Participation of Catholics in Political Life,"

Soon after his election, Pope Benedict strongly reiterated these themes.[15]

Silvestrini, however, stood for an overall liberal line, a line bitterly opposed to Ratzinger's.

Silvestrini, says Diat, could "in no way" accept Ratzinger's election.[16]

* * *

In 2007, another mysterious object slipped out from the shadows. It was *Confession d'un Cardinal,* a French memoir by a retired cardinal who identified himself as a good friend of Martini and Kasper.[17]

One day in 2005, over a spaghetti dinner at the Antica Taverna restaurant, the book's mysterious cardinal told his French interviewer, Olivier Le Gendre, why he would not have voted for Ratzinger at that year's conclave.[18]

There were three reasons, the mysterious cardinal said.

First, he would not have voted for Ratzinger because of his age. Ratzinger, the new bishop of Rome, was over seventy-five years old at his election—when bishops are supposed to resign at seventy-five, the mysterious cardinal said.[19]

Vatican website, November 24, 2002, https://www.vatican.va/roman_cu
ria/congregations/cfaith/documents/rc_con_cfaith_doc_20021124_poli
tica_en.html.

15 "Address of His Holiness Benedict XVI to the Members of the European People's Party on the Occasion of the Study Days on Europe," Vatican website, March 30, 2006, http://www.vatican.va/content/benedict-xvi/en/speeches/2006/march/documents/hf_ben-xvi_spe_20060330_eu-parli
amentarians.html.

16 Diat, *L'Homme,* 97.

17 Olivier Le Gendre, *Confession d'un Cardinal* (Paris: JC Lattès, 2007), NOOK.

18 Le Gendre, *Confession d'un Cardinal,* 65.

19 Le Gendre, *Confession d'un Cardinal,* 65.

Second, the mysterious cardinal would not have voted for Ratzinger because of his profession. The Church did not need a professional theologian to condemn the world, seeing nothing but a grim dictatorship of relativism. The Church needed a pope who, inspired by the historian's vision, would instead show the world how the Church herself had changed.[20]

Thus came what Fr. Claude Barthe calls the central thesis of this "post-Benedict XVI" manifesto: secularization must be accepted as the means for destroying an old, Tridentine model of the Church.[21]

Finally, the mysterious cardinal would not have voted for Ratzinger because he was a European.[22] For the mysterious cardinal had identified a certain non-European as an alternative to the German.

The mysterious cardinal referenced a period of about two and a half years in which he and unnamed others grappled with the question of John Paul II's succession. He and his collaborators thought of the possibility of a pope from Latin America, with European roots.[23]

"And we thought of Cardinal Bergoglio," he said.[24]

Bergoglio, the mysterious cardinal continued, represented a kind of succession from Martini. And Bergoglio proved himself when, by the conclave's third ballot, he made a "significant breakthrough" with thirty-five votes.[25]

"This point is to be remembered for the future, in case the pontificate of Benedict XVI does not last long," said the

20 Le Gendre, *Confession d'un Cardinal*, 65, 81–82.
21 Claude Barthe, "Y a-t-il une Opposition Romaine au Pape Benoit XVI?" *L'Homme Nouveau*, January 2009.
22 Le Gendre, *Confession d'un Cardinal*, 65.
23 Le Gendre, *Confession d'un Cardinal*, 114–115.
24 Le Gendre, *Confession d'un Cardinal*, 115.
25 Le Gendre, *Confession d'un Cardinal*, 121.

mysterious cardinal. "Indeed, [Jorge] Mario Bergoglio is only sixty-eight years old."[26]

* * *

Was the mysterious cardinal actually Silvestrini attempting to launch the next installment of his campaigns against Pope Benedict? Diat and others saw evidence of Silvestrini's hand in *Confession d'un Cardinal*.[27]

The similarities between the mysterious cardinal and Silvestrini indeed seem obvious. Both were retired cardinals over eighty years old. Both were made cardinals when they were about sixty. Both had worked in the Curia and been close to John Paul II. Both were friends with Martini and Kasper and supporters of Bergoglio. Both admitted, in various ways, their disappointment over Benedict's election.

Then there were the small details that eerily mapped onto Silvestrini's character. For instance, the mysterious cardinal said he had planned for the conclave with others for specifically two and a half years. Silvestrini joined the mafia in 2003—meaning he plotted with them for approximately two and a half years, from January 2003 (the time of the group's annual meeting) to April 2005 (the time of the conclave).

Certainly, some details, such as the cardinals' exact ages, did not perfectly line up. And yet one wondered: was there a deliberate effort to half-unveil, half-obscure the cardinal's identity? One thought of how, according to Barthe and others, it was none other than Silvestrini who leaked the photo of the mafia's secret pre-conclave meeting ("A Visit Enjoyed by Friends").[28]

26　Le Gendre, *Confession d'un Cardinal*, 121.

27　Diat, *L'Homme*, 101.

28　For one translation of Barthe's article in *L'Homme Nouveau* (January 31, 2009), see "¿Una Voluntad Hostil a Benedicto XVI? Quiénes, Cómo," *Catalunya Religió*, August 31, 2012, https://www.catalunyareligio.cat/es

And yet Silvestrini revealed the photo primarily in a small magazine run by his own residence[29]—as if there was something in him that both longed to confess and could not fully do so.

At one point in their meal at the Antica Taverna, the mysterious cardinal, who may have been Silvestrini, alluded to the "antagonistic tendencies" separating the revolutionaries from Ratzinger.[30]

Le Gendre asked for some examples.

"Three, since you are testing me," the mysterious cardinal said.[31]

/node/157212.

29   The photo was published in the May 2005 issue of the Villa Nazareth's bulletin. See Philippe Levillain, *Le Moment Benoît XVI* (Fayard, 2008), 146, footnote 15, NOOK.

30   Le Gendre, *Confession d'un Cardinal*, 62.

31   Le Gendre, *Confession d'un Cardinal*, 63.

3

Martini

O ne disagreement with Ratzinger—said the mysterious cardinal of *Confession d'un Cardinal*—concerned the issue of
councils.

Martini, the mysterious cardinal's good friend, thought it
would be good to call a new council. But Ratzinger had several times resisted the notion. For, said the mysterious cardinal,
even if he said it "less openly," Ratzinger thought the Church
was struggling to control various aberrations following the
Second Vatican Council.[1]

The mysterious cardinal left it at that, but he was broaching
a topic that touched Martini deeply.

He was speaking of the dream.

* * *

Born outside of Turin in 1927, Martini lived in that liminal
historical moment when one world starts to fade and another
struggles to be born. Many years later, Martini would remember how his pious mother would wake him up on First Fridays

---

1   Olivier Le Gendre, *Confession d'un Cardinal* (Paris: JC Lattès, 2007), 65,
     NOOK.

so he could receive Holy Communion. He would remember being ten and knowing that he had to devote his life wholly to God; he would remember, at age seventeen, getting on the train to become a Jesuit.[2]

Overall, the pre-conciliar Church of his youth, Martini later said, was heavy, boring.[3]

Martini wanted to scale mountains.

When he was a boy, his father, an expert hiker, would take him out to ascend high peaks. Later, the boy—by nature shy, bookish, and afraid of life—would run off with some bread and cheese and seek out a somewhat dangerous ascent. Mountain climbing was fringed with danger; "people even do it because it is risky, because they are afraid not to do it," Martini liked to say. Then he would speak of the "sudden joy" of glimpsing the summit and "having conquered, a joy impossible to those who reach the top in the comfort of a chair-lift."[4]

Something else made Martini's blue eyes sparkle—as if it, too, marked the conquest of a summit.

It was the Second Vatican Council.

A respected biblical scholar in his thirties, Martini did not participate in the council. But he would later speak about how it marked the greatest period of his life, not just because he was young, but because the air had suddenly grown fresh.[5]

---

2   For an overview of Martini's early life, see Aldo Maria Valli, *Storia di un Uomo: Ritratto di Carlo Maria Martini* (Milan: Ancora, 2011); and *Vedete, Sono Uno di Voi: Carlo Maria Martini*, directed by Ermanno Olmi (Italy: Rai Cinema, 2017), DVD.

3   Olmi, *Vedete, Sono Uno di Voi*.

4   Valli, *Storia di un Uomo*, loc. 470 of 3334; Carlo Maria Martini, *Perseverance in Trials: Reflections on Job* (United States: Liturgical Press, 1992), 131.

5   Valli, *Storia di un Uomo*, loc. 2879 of 3334.

And one day, Martini would emerge as a spiritual heir to a key Vatican II revolutionary: Fr. Karl Rahner, SJ.[6]

A German theologian suspected of heterodoxy in the time of Pope Pius XII, Rahner was arguably the council's "most powerful man."[7] And one of Rahner's key collaborators in those days was none other than a young, brilliant theologian named Joseph Ratzinger.

In October 1962—the month of the council's beginning—Rahner secretly met with a group including Ratzinger, the personal theological advisor of Cardinal Josef Frings. A plan was being hatched to submit an opposing "Ratzinger-Rahner schema" in place of an official council schema.[8] In those days, a "coup" began to form around Ratzinger.[9]

At one private planning session, Ratzinger dramatically challenged various conciliar schemata—helping to divert the council from its course. "He must have known he was playing with fire," says his biographer, Peter Seewald.[10]

For Ratzinger's presentation against the council's schemata had emboldened his cardinal, Frings. Later, in the council hall, Frings helped lead a first insurrection against the event's electoral procedures. "Happy coup and daring violation of the rules!" cried one progressive cardinal.[11]

6   For a discussion of Rahner's influence on Martini, see Roberto de Mattei, "The Second Vatican Council: A Story Now Being Written," *Catholic Family News*, May 22, 2019, https://catholicfamilynews.com/blog/2019 /05/22/the-second-vatican-council-a-story-now-being-written/.

7   Herbert Vorgrimler, *Understanding Karl Rahner: An Introduction to His Life and Thought* (New York: Crossroad, 1986), 88–92, 99.

8   Peter Seewald, *Benedict XVI: A Life (Vol. 1)*, trans. Dinah Livingstone (London: Bloomsbury, 2020), 442, Kindle. See also Roberto de Mattei, *The Second Vatican Council: An Unwritten Story* (Fitzwilliam, NH: Loreto Publications, 2013), loc. 6531 of 16572, Kindle.

9   Seewald, *Benedict XVI: A Life*, 431.

10 Seewald, *Benedict XVI: A Life*, 426–429.

11 Seewald, *Benedict XVI: A Life*, 434–437.

It was a heady moment. The revolutionaries felt their power. Soon, through a series of maneuvers, the innovators made headway on overturning the council's original schemata.[12]

Ultimately, according to progressive theologian Hans Küng, the Roman Curia "was able to stop any movement of reform"— though "not completely, but half-way."[13] This "half-way" revolution generated Vatican II's "ambivalent" and ambiguous documents.

For instance, after Rahner and others attacked the original schema on collegiality, some counter-revolutionaries warned Pope Paul VI that the new schema's ambiguous passages could, after the council, be interpreted in a radical way. As Fr. Ralph Wiltgen explains, collegiality, in its extreme form, stipulated that the pope "would be bound in conscience to request the opinion of the college of bishops before making a pronouncement."[14]

Ultimately, says Wiltgen, "one of the extreme liberals made the mistake of referring, in writing, to some of these ambiguous passages, and indicating how they would be interpreted after the Council."[15] Paul VI wept at the revolutionaries' deception. He announced that a preliminary note would rule out a liberal interpretation of the council's text. But according to de Mattei, the note was a precarious "compromise"—ambivalently placing papal primacy and episcopal collegiality on the same level.[16]

---

12   De Mattei, *The Second Vatican Council*, loc. 6522 of 16572.

13   Jerry Filteau, "Hans Kung Urges Peaceful Revolution Against Roman Absolutism," *National Catholic Reporter*, June 11, 2011, https://www.ncr online.org/news/parish/hans-kung-urges-peaceful-revolution-against -roman-absolutism.

14   Ralph Wiltgen, *The Inside Story of Vatican II: A Firsthand Account of the Council's Inner Workings* (Charlotte, NC: TAN Books, 2014), 346.

15   Wiltgen, *Inside Story of Vatican II*, 352.

16   Roberto de Mattei, "Tu es Petrus: True Devotion to the Chair of Saint Peter," *Catholic Family News*, April 10, 2018, https://catholicfamilynews .com/blog/2018/04/10/tu-es-petrus-true-devotion-to-the-chair-of-saint

That ambiguity and ambivalence were dangerous. Martini and others would exploit the danger to follow the freewheeling "spirit of Vatican II" up the mountain of revolution.

But in the meantime, Ratzinger began speaking sadly of the growing impression "that actually nothing was firm in the church, that everything was up for revision." "The genie was out of the bottle," says Seewald, "and almost no one was more alarmed about it than its driving force from Bavaria."[17]

* * *

But somewhere in snowy St. Gallen, Switzerland, just north of the Alps, a group called the Council of the European Bishops' Conferences (CCEE) helped keep the spirit of revolution alive.

Founded in 1971, the CCEE pursued decentralization—code for flouting Rome's authority. As journalist Maike Hickson puts it, "The leaders of the CCEE at the time tried to establish a parallel structure in defiance against Roman centralism, often not even asking Rome for permission for their actions." By 1974, for instance, the CCEE was already floating the possibility of opening up Holy Communion to the divorced and civilly remarried.[18]

From 1979 to 1986, the CCEE's president was a tall, hieratic monk-cardinal from England named Basil Hume.

One day in 1980, at a synod on the family, Hume dramatically announced he had fallen asleep—and dreamed. Hume saw the Church as "a pilgrim through history and through life," hastening "toward all truth" and yet limping along the road. Then

---

-peter/.

17   Seewald, *Benedict XVI: A Life*, 497.

18   Maike Hickson, "Evidence Pope Follows Blueprint to Change Church by Dissident Cardinal who Led St. Gallen 'Mafia,'" LifeSiteNews, March 29, 2019, https://www.lifesitenews.com/blogs/evidence-pope-follows-blueprint-to-change-church-by-dissident-cardinal-who-led-st.-gallen-mafia.

he saw that *Humanae Vitae*'s signposts were "weather-beaten" and in need of new paint.

"My dream became a nightmare," Hume cried, "for I saw the wrong paint being put upon the signposts, and the last state was worse than the first."[19]

That was how, in the conservative John Paul II era, the revolutionaries so often had to express themselves: in code. Just before the synod, Hume had tried to show the pope a report registering lay dissent against *Humanae Vitae*'s anti-contraception stance. The pope swept the paper away.[20]

Meanwhile, John Paul II's handpicked synodal relator, Ratzinger, "strenuously defended traditional positions on birth control and other issues of sexual morality," according to one vaticanista.[21]

But sitting in the audience, the new archbishop of Milan, Martini, felt captivated by Hume's dream.

"I can recall," he later said of Hume, "the words with which he began his address: 'I have had a dream!' It was his way of expressing, through symbols, the changes he believed were needed within the Church."[22]

Soon after meeting Hume, in 1981, Martini began speaking of his own dream. He dreamed of a "synodal" Church where power was transferred away from the papal center and toward the advisory body known as the synod of bishops. Synods— to borrow a phrase from Ross Douthat—seemed to offer

---

19   "Cardinal Had a Dream," *The Anchor*, October 23, 1980.

20   Clifford Longley, "Hume's Mission Impossible," *The Tablet*, November 20, 1999, 1572–1573.

21   John Allen Jr., *The Rise of Benedict XVI: The Inside Story of How the Pope Was Elected and Where He Will Take the Church* (New York: Doubleday, 2007), 141, NOOK.

22   Carlo Maria Martini, "A Boon to Us All," in *Basil Hume: By His Friends*, ed. Carolyn Butler (London: Harper Collins, 1999), 76.

progressives a "mechanism for changing the Church's answers to some questions."[23]

But because Pope John Paul II tightly controlled his synods, Martini had to keep his plans "under the category of 'dream,'" says his biographer, Marco Garzonio. As Garzonio says of Martini: "As a prudent Jesuit, he had understood that his arguments did not constitute material welcome to the leadership. He presented his ideas as a goal that was perhaps a long way away, but he was not silent."[24]

In the meantime, Martini and Hume became great friends, and Martini began engaging with the CCEE. Martini grew in power. In 1986, he succeeded Hume as the CCEE's president. By the early 1990s, according to CCEE secretary Ivo Fürer, the Vatican had a "fear" of Martini.[25]

In 1990—when the pope began planning a special synod on Europe—he did not inform Martini. Martini—who had already started meeting in St. Gallen to organize a CCEE symposium on European unity—"was very surprised" by the pope's synod preparations.[26] At the synod, "one noticed an enmity against the strong personality" of Martini, with some even speaking of an "anti-Martini synod," says Fürer.[27]

---

23   Ross Douthat, *To Change the Church: Pope Francis and the Future of Catholicism* (New York: Simon & Schuster, 2018), 102–103, Kindle.

24   Sandro Magister, "Martini Pope. The Dream Come True," *L'Espresso*, October 15, 2013, http://chiesa.espresso.repubblica.it/articolo/1350623bdc 4.html?eng=y.

25   Maike Hickson, "Swiss Bishop Describes Struggle Between John Paul II and Saint Gallen Group," LifeSiteNews, November 22, 2019, https://www .lifesitenews.com/blogs/swiss-bishop-describes-struggle-between-john -paul-ii-and-saint-gallen-group.

26   Ivo Fürer, "Cardinal Hume's Influence in Europe," in *Basil Hume: Ten Years On*, ed. William Charles (London: Burns and Oates, 2009), 146.

27   Hickson, "Swiss Bishop Describes Struggle."

Eventually, following a private audience with Martini, the pope changed the mechanism for selecting the CCEE's leader. Martini had effectively been ousted.

Down Martini came from the mountain, missing the summit, toppled.

* * *

But like a center of gravity, St. Gallen drew Martini back. In the mid-1990s, Martini launched his mafia, hosted by Fürer, then bishop of St. Gallen.

Near St. Gallen, in eastern Switzerland, there is a Benedictine monastery called Fischingen. In pictures, you can see it huddled among the trees, its clocks popping with brilliant turquoise as they mark the inexorable march of time.

There, the St. Gallen mafia convened for their January 1999 meeting.

As Danneels's biography notes, besides Martini and Fürer, the key personalities of this initial group were the Germans Kasper and Lehmann. Together, the group tackled key topics—from ecclesial centralism and collegiality to the development of the priestly ministry and sexual morality. Each year, one member gave the annual presentation—and this year, it was Martini's turn.[28]

He told the others he wanted a new council.

Danneels, who had just joined the group that year, listened sympathetically but critically. He was worried about logistics—questions about finances and linguistic barriers and the challenges of assembling some five thousand bishops. He remained pragmatic, skeptical.[29]

---

28 Jürgen Mettepenningen and Karim Schelkens, *Godfried Danneels: Biographie* (Antwerpen: Uitgeverij Polis, 2015), 449, https://pure.uvt.nl/ws /portalfiles/portal/28312169/Danneels_Polis_FR.pdf.

29 Mettepenningen and Schelkens, *Godfried Danneels*, 449.

But like a spark hungry to grow, Martini's dream lived on.

Later that year—on October 7, 1999, before a synod of bishops—Martini recalled how the now-deceased Hume had once opened his synodal intervention with the words: "I had a dream."

Martini said he, too, had a dream—or, rather, several dreams.

Martini focused on his third dream, recalling the joyful return of the disciples of Emmaus to Jerusalem. Channeling that spirit, Martini dreamed of periodic convocations focusing on certain "doctrinal and disciplinary knots."

"In general," he said, "the key task is the deepening and the development of the ecclesiology of communion of Vatican II." "Another," he said, "is to address the deficit—in some places quite dramatic—of ordained ministers."

"Others," he continued, "include the position of women in society and the church, the participation of the laity in some ministerial responsibilities, sexuality, the discipline of marriage, the practice of penance, the relationship with the sister Orthodox churches (and in a more generalized manner, the need to revive ecumenical hope), and the need to work out the relationship between democracy and values, between civil laws and moral law."[30]

Then he exhorted everyone to pray that, through the intercession of Mary, they might be able to discern how and when such dreams could come true.

Media reports said he had called for a new council; Martini said he had not. What he had laid out, as vaticanista Sandro Magister notes, was a blueprint for a succession of synods, on topics ranging from Communion for the divorced and civilly

---

30   John Allen Jr., "Martini Calls for a New Council…Almost," *The National Catholic Reporter*, October 11, 1999, https://natcath.org/NCR_Online /documents/JA10-11.htm.

remarried to the ordination of married men.[31] It was a program for getting the Church into a state of "permanent" synodality—what some critics might call "permanent revolution."[32]

But according to Garzonio, Martini was bitter.

He was bitter because most synodal fathers opposed his vision.

He was bitter because, as the dawn of a new millennium drew near, the old cardinal still had to speak of a far-off "dream."[33]

✳ ✳ ✳

In December 2005, Benedict XVI stood before the Roman Curia to assess the legacy of Vatican II. There, the man who had helped spark a revolution now quoted St. Basil, who had compared another council's aftermath to a naval battle in the blackness of a storm.[34]

"Harsh rises the cry of the combatants encountering one another in dispute; already all the Church is almost full of the inarticulate screams, the unintelligible noises, rising from the ceaseless agitations that divert the right rule of the doctrine of true religion," said Pope Benedict, quoting Basil.[35]

---

31   Sandro Magister, "The Next Synod Is Already in the Works. On Married Priests," *L'Espresso*, December 9, 2015, http://chiesa.espresso.repubblica .it/articolo/1351189bdc4.html?eng=y.

32   See Edward Pentin, "Cardinal Baldisseri Praises Synodality But Concept is Causing Concern," *The National Catholic Register*, December 14, 2016, https://www.ncregister.com/blog/edward-pentin/cardinal-baldisseri -praises-synodality-but-concerns-grow.

33   Magister, "Martini Pope."

34   Sandro Magister, "Pope Ratzinger Certifies the Council—The Real One," *L'Espresso*, December 23, 2005, http://chiesa.espresso.repubblica.it/artico lo/44072bdc4.html.

35   Quoted in Magister, "Pope Ratzinger Certifies the Council." Basil's quo-tation is from *De Spiritu Sancto*, XXX.

"It is not a dramatic description such as this that we would want to apply to the post-Council situation," Benedict said, "but some of what has happened does reflect itself in it."[36]

Then Benedict explained the importance of tethering any interpretation of the council to its texts, read in continuity with Tradition. And yet his very decision to quote Basil seemed to upstage the rest of the speech, conjuring the image of groping in darkness and chaos after the council.

Martini's dream was still not to be.

---

36 Magister, "Pope Ratzinger Certifies the Council."

4

Kasper

The revolutionaries' second area of contention with Ratzinger—the mysterious cardinal of *Confession d'un Cardinal* said—was highly technical.

Kasper, the mysterious cardinal's friend, had publicly debated Ratzinger over whether the universal Church held priority over the local one. In a circumlocutory and esoteric way, the mysterious cardinal explained how Kasper wanted more autonomy for local churches, while Ratzinger wanted their subordination to Rome.[1]

Then the mysterious cardinal spoke no more of the issue.

But Kasper would later elaborate on how "difficult" the situation with Ratzinger had been. He would recall sitting one day at a 2000 Vatican symposium only to hear Ratzinger sharply take issue with Kasper's 1999 publication on local churches. "A third of the lecture critically took issue with my position in the cited essay, explicitly mentioning my name," said Kasper. "This was not the reception into the Roman Curia that I had wished for."[2]

---

1   Olivier Le Gendre, *Confession d'un Cardinal* (Paris: JC Lattès, 2007), 63–64, NOOK.

2   Walter Kasper, *Essential Spiritual Writings*, ed. Robert A. Krieg and Patri-

For Kasper, it would be a long road toward revolution.

*　*　*

Born in 1933 in southwest Germany, Kasper was constantly walking toward the new. He grew up in the static, aura-filled world of Pius XII. "Pius XII was a sacrosanct authority who was honored," Kasper said. "We would never have thought of criticizing him." Then, when the pope died, "all of a sudden there came to the fore pent up questions which had been previously discussed only in the smallest circles."[3]

Many of those "pent up questions" came from Fr. Karl Rahner, the Jesuit whose work had been censored under Pius XII on suspicion of heterodoxy. Many years later, Kasper would still remember Rahner's bracing lectures at his university. Kasper would recall how, perusing Rahner's *Theological Investigations* for the first time, he was "totally fascinated" and began reading an essay on dogma while walking on the street.[4]

Those were the moments that transported Kasper to another realm, that swept him up like a wave. Listening to the radio with some friends one night, a young Fr. Kasper heard that John XXIII had convoked the Second Vatican Council.

"We could not believe our ears," Kasper said. "It was like lightning from a blue sky."[5]

From 1964 to 1970, Kasper served as a professor of dogmatics at the University of Münster, where Rahner and his young assistant, Karl Lehmann, likewise arrived.

---

cia C. Bellm (Maryknoll, NY: Orbis, 2016), loc. 2104 of 2844, Kindle.

3   Kasper, *Essential Spiritual Writings*, loc. 2034–2042 of 2844.

4   Kasper, *Essential Spiritual Writings*, loc. 2049 of 2844.

5   Kristin M. Colberg and Robert A. Krieg, eds., *The Theology of Cardinal Walter Kasper: Speaking Truth in Love* (Collegeville, MN: Liturgical Press, 2010), 278, Kindle.

"Rahner was one of the great thinkers before, during, and after the Council," Kasper said. But Rahner "was increasingly dissatisfied with a post-conciliar development that, he argued, was both lagging and backward looking."[6]

As Vatican II drew to a close, Rahner gave a lecture calling the council "the beginning of a beginning." He was, said Kasper, cautiously pursuing further developments.[7]

In 1967, Rahner helped the German bishops draft a letter declaring that "the Church can be subject to error and has in fact erred" in the past. Rahner then used the text to argue that *Humanae Vitae*'s stance against contraception was not irreformable.[8]

Then, in his 1972 manifesto *The Shape of the Church to Come*, Rahner dreamed of what the future Church would look like.[9] He was dreaming of what Stefano Fontana calls a "new Church"—centered on "surrender to the world."[10]

Rahner dreamed of a Church where it was "not clear" that the divorced and civilly remarried could "in no circumstances" receive Holy Communion. He dreamed of a Church with less "moralizing" and more formation of consciences.[11]

---

6   Walter Kasper, *The Catholic Church: Nature, Reality, and Mission* (London: Bloomsbury, 2015), 6.

7   Colberg and Krieg, *The Theology of Cardinal Walter Kasper*, 281.

8   Eamonn Conway, "Rahner's 'Tough Love' for the Church: Structural Change as Task and Opportunity," in *Karl Rahner: Theologian for the Twenty-First Century*, ed. Padraic Conway and Fainche Ryan (Oxford: Peter Lang, 2010), 149.

9   Karl Rahner, *The Shape of the Church to Come* (London: S.P.C.K., 1974).

10   Stefano Fontana, *La Nuova Chiesa di Karl Rahner: Il Teologo che ha Insegnato ad Arrendersi al Mondo* (Verona: Fede & Cultura, 2017).

11   Rahner, *Shape of the Church*, 95, 67–68.

He dreamed of a Church where it was "obvious" that celibacy "must not be imposed" amidst priestly shortages—and where there was "no reason in principle" to ban women's ordination.[12]

Rahner dreamed of a Church that implemented synodality—the right of priests and laity to cooperate "in a deliberative and not merely consultative way" in Church decision-making.[13]

And he dreamed of a Church where it was not so clear what the possibilities were for Christians regarding "the state's penal laws" against abortion. Since "no political party in practice is so completely Christian in each and every respect," it was "not so easy to say when a party can no longer rely on the support of Christians and Catholics."[14]

Communion for the divorced and civilly remarried, the autonomy of conscience, synodality, the ordination of married men and women, the possibility of voting for pro-abortion politicians—these were the dreams of the man who might be called the father of the St. Gallen mafia.[15]

* * *

The revolutionaries started with priestly celibacy.

In 1970, Rahner and Lehmann (a future member of the Gallen group) devised a memorandum calling for a "serious investigation" of the law of celibacy in the Latin rite. Lacking

---

12   Rahner, *Shape of the Church*, 110, 114.

13   Rahner, *Shape of the Church*, 121.

14   Rahner, *Shape of the Church*, 95.

15   For Rahner's link to Martini, see "Remnant in Rome: Michael Matt Interviews Roberto de Mattei," *The Remnant*, February 26, 2019, https://remnantnewspaper.com/web/index.php/articles/item/4357-remnant-in-rome-michael-matt-interviews-roberto-de-mattei; and Roberto de Mattei, "The Second Vatican Council: A Story Now Being Written," *Catholic Family News*, May 22, 2019, https://catholicfamilynews.com/blog/2019/05/22/the-second-vatican-council-a-story-now-being-written/.

enough priests, the Church "quite simply has a responsibility to take up certain modifications," said the text.[16]

Kasper signed the memo. Ratzinger signed too—although many years later he would insist that he signed out of friendship and that the Rahnerian text could be interpreted in a traditional way.[17]

Ultimately, according to Vatican II revolutionary Hans Küng, Rahner was bitterly disappointed when the German episcopate gave the cold shoulder to his carefully worded memorandum on clerical celibacy. "Not only did the bishops fail to respond to the theologian's appeal to rethink the matter and take appropriate action; with two exceptions, they failed even to acknowledge receipts of the document," says Küng. As Küng points out, when Pope Paul VI had written a 1968 encyclical quashing further debate on celibacy, Rahner had (on orders from a cardinal) backed the Vatican line, and then had "painstakingly formulated his confidential memorandum two years later in a moderate, submissive voice." The episcopal rejection of this cautious 1970 intervention stung.[18]

Then, at a 1971 synod on the priesthood, a narrow majority of bishops voted against ordaining married men even in "particular cases." Decades after the synod, Lehmann would lament that "a fitting moment, a *kairos*, was missed."[19]

---

16 Dennis Coday, "Ratzinger, Rahner, et al. On Celibacy (1970)," *National Catholic Reporter*, January 30, 2012, https://www.ncronline.org/blogs/ncr-today/ratzinger-rahner-et-al-celibacy-1970.

17 Benedict XVI and Peter Seewald, *Last Testament: In His Own Words*, trans. Jacob Phillips (London: Bloomsbury, 2016), 157, Kindle.

18 Hans Küng, *Can We Save the Catholic Church?* (London: William Collins, 2013), 21–23, Kindle.

19 Maike Hickson, "Cardinal Lehmann's Memoirs: On His *Humanae Vitae* Dissent and the Conduct of Some Popes," OnePeterFive, March 14, 2018, https://onepeterfive.com/cardinal-lehmanns-memoirs-humanae-vitae-dissent-conduct-popes/.

Not to be deterred, Lehmann, Kasper, and Ratzinger seized the Rahnerian agenda to challenge the Church's proscription against Communion for the divorced and civilly remarried. Claiming they were not technically questioning the indissolubility of a sacramental marriage bond, Kasper, Lehmann, and Ratzinger wrote various texts in the 1970s asserting certain conditions for receiving the Eucharist. In a long-term second union with children, in which continence did not seem feasible, one could perform penance for the first marriage's irreparable breakdown, it was proposed.[20]

But as time passed, Ratzinger, the policeman's son, grew more and more concerned. As John Paul II's new prefect for the Congregation of the Doctrine of the Faith, Ratzinger produced a 1985 book-length interview that expressed both alarm and weariness with the revolutionary agenda.

"Admission of remarried divorced couples to the sacraments is constantly demanded," Ratzinger lamented at one point in *The Ratzinger Report*, as if sighing over the tired cry and all related demands. Then he sounded the alarm on the "dangers" of the present crisis, casting the post-conciliar period as a cauldron of "self-destruction" and "decadence."[21]

When the 1985 synod on the twenty-year legacy of Vatican II took place, Ratzinger's book dominated the discourse.

But officially, it was Kasper who, along with Danneels, was tasked with preparing the synod's texts. As Kasper later explained, his goal was to emphasize "balance," without joining

20   Nicholas Healy Jr., "The Merciful Gift of Indissolubility and the Question of Pastoral Care for Civilly Divorced and Remarried Catholics," *Communio* 41 (Summer 2014): 313, https://www.communio-icr.com/files/healy 41-2.pdf.

21   Joseph Ratzinger, *The Ratzinger Report: An Exclusive Interview on the State of the Church* (San Francisco: Ignatius Press, 1985), 87, 29–30.

in "the widespread lamentation."[22] So he and Danneels delivered a final synodal document that was, like certain key works of Vatican II, a compromise text, giving each side something to grasp.[23]

Patiently, Kasper kept walking toward the new.

✳ ✳ ✳

Kasper was prepared for change. In 1967, a young Fr. Kasper wrote:

> The God who is enthroned over the world and history as a changeless being is an offense to man. One must deny him for man's sake, because he claims for himself the dignity and honor that belong by right to man. . . . We must resist this God, however, not only for man's sake, but also for God's sake. He is not the true God at all, but rather a wretched idol. For a God who is only alongside of and above history, who is not himself history, is a finite God. If we call such a being God, then for the sake of the Absolute we must become absolute atheists. Such a God springs from a rigid worldview; he is the guarantor of the status quo and the enemy of the new.[24]

"An enemy of the new," a "wretched idol"—the passage scrawled, in big letters, a bald manifesto against divine immutability. Kasper was trying to make the God "enthroned over the world" subject to the undulating waters of history.

22 Colberg and Krieg, *The Theology of Walter Kasper*, 283.

23 Jürgen Mettepenningen and Karim Schelkens, *Godfried Danneels: Biographie* (Antwerpen: Uitgeverij Polis, 2015), 219–220, https://pure.uvt.nl/ws/portalfiles/portal/28312169/Danneels_Polis_FR.pdf.

24 Quoted in Mathew McCusker, "The Grave Problems Remaining in the Final Synod Report," LifeSiteNews, May 13, 2015, https://www.lifesitenews.com/opinion/the-grave-problems-remaining-in-the-final-synod-report.

"In this passage," says Matthew McCusker, "Kasper explicitly identifies the immutable nature of God as 'the guarantor
of the status quo.' In other words it is necessary for God to be
mutable in order that the natural and social order can itself be
considered open to change. If God Himself is subject to change
then everything else must also be mutable. By enchaining God
to history and to change Kasper is subordinating Him to human
ideas of 'progress.'"[25]

Which brought into view what vaticanista Edward Pentin
calls "a strong criticism of Cardinal Kasper's view of history,
one many critics have seen as Hegelian: that it is an evolution-
ary approach." Such a view "was manifested in the heresy of
Modernism, which made the understanding of divine truths
subject to changes in human nature and society."[26]

"If you have a concept of history like Kasper has, everything
and anything is possible," comments scholar Thomas Stark.
"Because what was important yesterday is maybe of no value
today."[27]

In 1993, Kasper, Lehmann, and another German bishop
resumed their crusade for the new. They carved a local opening
for Communion for the divorced and civilly remarried.

"Such a decision [to receive the Holy Eucharist]," they said,
"can only be made by the individual in a personal review of
his or her conscience and by no one else. However, he or she
will be in need of the clarifying assistance and the unbiased

25   McCusker, "The Grave Problems."

26   Edward Pentin, *The Rigging of a Vatican Synod?* (San Francisco: Ignatius
       Press, 2015), loc. 495 of 3138, Kindle.

27   Edward Pentin, "Understanding Cardinal Walter Kasper," July 11, 2015,
       The National Catholic Register, https://www.ncregister.com/news/unders
       tanding-cardinal-walter-kasper.

accompaniment of a church officeholder. . . . The priest will respect the judgment of the individual's conscience."[28]

In 1994, Ratzinger's Congregation for the Doctrine of the Faith shut down the pastoral experiment. "If the divorced are remarried civilly, they find themselves in a situation that objectively contravenes God's law. Consequently, they cannot receive Holy Communion as long as this situation persists," Ratzinger's office said.[29]

Then, in the mid-1990s, Kasper walked into the ranks of the St. Gallen mafia.

Before the 2005 conclave, dressed in a red skullcap and black coat and carrying a briefcase, Kasper was filmed walking through the streets of Rome looking radiant.

The bells rang.

Kasper checked his watch.

Smiling, he kept walking.[30]

* * *

On April 17, 2005, Kasper delivered a pre-conclave homily at Santa Maria in Trastevere.

"We are about to elect a new pope in next week's conclave," he said, stressing the need for a "pastor" with understanding. Then he launched what many understood as an attack against Ratzinger.[31]

---

28 Quoted in Charles Curran and Julie Hanlon Rubio, eds., *Marriage: Readings in Moral Theology No. 15* (New York: Paulist Press, 2009), 392.

29 Quoted in Carl Bunderson, "Scholars: No, Benedict XVI Doesn't Support Kasper in Synod Debates," *Catholic News Agency*, November 25, 2014, https://www.catholicnewsagency.com/news/31002/scholars-no-benedict-xvi-doesnt-support-kasper-in-synod-debates.

30 Associated Press Archive, "Cardinals Arrive for Pre-Conclave Meeting," YouTube video, 3:22, July 21, 2015, https://www.youtube.com/watch?v=dDPy-maF__0.

31 John Allen Jr., *The Rise of Benedict XVI: The Inside Story of How the Pope*

"Just as it is forbidden to clone others, it is not possible to clone Pope John Paul II," Kasper said. "Let's not search for someone who is too scared of doubt and secularity in the modern world."[32]

But when Ratzinger was elected pope, Kasper kept moving forward, implying Benedict XVI would walk with him.

"Clearly he's not a clone of John Paul II," Kasper said of Benedict. "I think he's a pastoral man. He will be a pastoral pope."[33]

Later that year, the fathers of a synod on the Eucharist voted against opening up Communion to the divorced and civilly remarried.

"I cannot imagine that the discussion is closed," Kasper said. He insisted that the synod's decision was "not the final result" and that calls for change had been heard. Then he reminded everyone that Pope Benedict still had to write his post-synodal exhortation.[34]

In 2007, Benedict's *Sacramentum Caritatis* shut down the Kasper proposal once again.

And yet something ominous hung in the air.

"He will surprise everyone," Kasper had said after Benedict's election.[35]

Was Elected and Where He Will Take the Church (New York: Doubleday, 2007), 96, NOOK.

32 Allen, *The Rise of Benedict XVI*, 96.
33 Allen, *The Rise of Benedict XVI*, 120.
34 "Cardinal Kasper Questions Synod Conclusion on Divorce and Communion," *Catholic Culture*, October 24, 2005, https://www.catholicculture.org/news/features/index.cfm?recnum=40341.
35 "Cardinal Kasper: Benedict XVI will be Pope of Reconciliation and Peace," *Catholic News Agency*, April 21, 2005, https://www.catholicnewsagency.com/news/cardinal_kasper_benedict_xvi_will_be_pope_of_reconciliation_and_peace.

5

Danneels

Another revolutionary point of antagonism, the mysterious cardinal of *Confession d'un Cardinal* said, had to do with condoms.

Not long before his death, Pope John Paul II had reaffirmed that the sole methods to fight the spread of AIDS were abstinence and marital fidelity. Danneels, however, publicly presented condoms as an alternative to those who could not respect those rules. Strangely, Pope John Paul II's personal theologian, Cardinal Georges Cottier, agreed with Danneels that condoms could be licit in some circumstances.[1]

The mysterious cardinal stopped there, but he was gesturing toward a secretive underground force.

* * *

The dutiful eldest son of a Belgian schoolteacher, Danneels seemed an unlikely candidate for the shadow-world of

---

1   Olivier Le Gendre, *Confession d'un Cardinal* (Paris: JC Lattès, 2007), 63, NOOK. See also "Papal Theologian Weighs Condom Use Against AIDS," *Catholic Culture*, February 1, 2005, https://www.catholicculture.org/news /features/index.cfm?recnum=34990.

St. Gallen. He grew up in a quaint village in rural western Belgium. His father wrote manuals about breeding chickens while the son played games with birdsongs or served Mass early in the morning.[2]

It was a sunny pre-conciliar world, and it seemed natural that the bright boy who was fascinated by the candles of the liturgy would one day set off to study for the priesthood at the Catholic University of Louvain.

Then came the Second Vatican Council. Danneels, a young priest-scholar, watched the event's Belgian contingent—and learned.

Cardinal Leo Joseph Suenens was a Belgian progressive who chose Professor Gerard Philips for his assistant. Philips, as Suenens said, "personified a kind of *via media*" that others would not find "threatening." "I always strove to reach an agreement," Philips said. "People prefer a battle: it is a pity."[3]

It was a pity because, while some die-hards called for rejecting a conciliar schema outright, Philips introduced subtle changes in wording that utterly changed a passage's meaning. This Belgian "middle way," says historian Roberto de Mattei, "turned out to be the most effective way to assure" the revolutionaries' success.[4]

Suenens, meanwhile, suggested a commission on birth control to Pope John XXIII—and then tapped many of its members. Taking the floor one day at the council, Suenens called for the Church to "follow the progress of science" to avoid another

---

2   For a discussion of Danneels's early life, see Godfried Danneels, *Confidences d'un Cardinal* (Bruxelles: Racine, 2009), and Jürgen Mettepenningen and Karim Schelkens, *Godfried Danneels: Biographie* (Antwerpen: Uitgeverij Polis, 2015), https://pure.uvt.nl/ws/portalfiles/portal/283121 69/Danneels_Polis_FR.pdf.

3   Roberto de Mattei, *The Second Vatican Council: An Unwritten Story* (Fitzwilliam, NH: Loreto Publications, 2013), loc. 8681 of 16572, Kindle.

4   De Mattei, *The Second Vatican Council*, loc. 8681 of 16572.

"Galileo trial." Rapt applause broke out. It had been scripted beforehand by one of Suenens's fellow conspirators.[5]

According to de Mattei, Pope Paul VI scolded Suenens for his indiscriminate speech.

But it was too late.

Something shadowy and relentless was rising up. A liberal lobby leaked the rumor that the birth control commission had overturned the contraception ban. "The belief that Paul VI had changed the doctrine of the Church on birth control spread throughout public opinion," says de Mattei.[6]

In July 1968, Danneels, vacationing as a tourist in Italy, watched as Pope Paul VI released *Humanae Vitae*, which reaffirmed the Church's ancient ban on contraception. Then Danneels watched as Suenens and Philips gained public credibility by undermining the papal text.[7]

The Belgian "middle way"—the way of plotting compromise—had ended in open dissent. In August 1968, the Belgian bishops, led by Suenens, issued a declaration on *Humanae Vitae* that de Mattei calls "a model of rebellion for other episcopates."[8]

* * *

In 1979, Danneels—the cautious man of balance—was tapped as Suenens's successor.

He opened with discretion.

At the 1980 synod on the family, where Basil Hume spoke obliquely about a "dream" involving innovations to *Humanae*

5   Roberto de Mattei, "The Two Revolutions of '68," *Catholic Family News*, May 21, 2018, https://catholicfamilynews.com/blog/2018/05/21/the-two -revolutions-of-68/.

6   De Mattei, "The Two Revolutions."

7   Mettepenningen and Schelkens, *Godfried Danneels*, 97.

8   De Mattei, "The Two Revolutions."

Vitae, Danneels listened carefully before speaking. Then the schoolteacher's son spoke discreetly about balancing "ideals" with pastoral "realities" on contraception.[9]

One day, Hume, leader of the St. Gallen-based CCEE, placed a call to Danneels. The CCEE president invited Danneels to participate in the group, and Danneels became a popular figure in St. Gallen. Danneels soon met Martini, and both became close friends and cardinals in 1983.[10]

At the 1985 synod on Vatican II's legacy, Danneels again listened. But, says a vaticanista, "Danneels became so sick of answering questions about *The Ratzinger Report* during a press conference that he snapped, 'This is not a synod about a book, it's a synod on the Council!'"[11]

Ultimately, Danneels and Kasper, the synod's main architects, found a way to move past Ratzinger's tone of lamentation. The future mafia members melded their own progressive stances with various compromise proposals. Their final text spoke both of conservative themes and of liberal themes, both of a catechism and of collegiality, and John Paul II pronounced himself satisfied. According to Danneels's biography, the Danneels-Kasper document was a masterful synthesis, leaving all parties satisfied and no door closed for the liberals.[12]

In the early 1990s, when Pope John Paul II effectively ousted Martini from the presidency of the CCEE, Danneels stepped back from the group.[13] But by January 1999, Danneels was

---

9   Sean O'Riordan, "The Synod on the Family, 1980," *The Furrow* 12 (Dec. 1980): 759–777. See also Mettepenningen and Schelkens, *Godfried Danneels*, 174.

10   Mettepenningen and Schelkens, *Godfried Danneels*, 207.

11   John Allen Jr., *The Rise of Benedict XVI: The Inside Story of How the Pope Was Elected and Where He Will Take the Church* (New York: Doubleday, 2007), 131, NOOK.

12   Mettepenningen and Schelkens, *Godfried Danneels*, 219–220.

13   Marcantonio Colonna [Henry Sire], *The Dictator Pope: The Inside Story*

back in the St. Gallen area for his first mafia meeting. There, at the monastery of Fischingen, an underground force made its plans.[14]

The mafia's *modus operandi*, according to Danneels's biography, was to plot privately at first—then follow up with public, incremental action.[15] And by 2000, according to one of Danneels's biographers, the mafia was thinking "more strategically about what was going to happen to the Church after John Paul II."[16]

In January 2000, just as he was finishing his time with the Gallen group, Karl Lehmann set off a firestorm. "I personally believe that the Holy Father is capable of bravely confessing, 'I can no longer adequately carry out my role as is necessary,'" said Lehmann in a radio interview.[17]

"The Pope is Tired. Resign," ran one Italian headline on Lehmann's remarks.

In October, Danneels's turn came. Referring to the retirement of bishops at age seventy-five, Danneels said, "I wouldn't be surprised if the pope also retired after 2000. He absolutely wanted to reach the Jubilee year, but I believe he would retire afterward."[18]

The remarks from Danneels and Lehmann were, as James Hitchcock puts it, "trial balloons" by which "speakers 'predict'"

of the Francis Papacy (Washington, DC: Regenery, 2017), 6, Kindle.

14 Mettepenningen and Schelkens, *Godfried Danneels*, 449.

15 Mettepenningen and Schelkens, *Godfried Danneels*, 450.

16 Jeanne Smits, "Cardinal Danneels Admits Being Part of Clerical 'Mafia' that Plotted Francis's Election," LifeSiteNews, September 25, 2015, https://www.lifesitenews.com/news/cardinal-danneels-admits-being-part-of-clerical-mafia-that-plotted-francis.

17 Bob Harvey, "Vatican Rejects Call for Pope to Step Down," *The Ottawa Citizen*, January 11, 2000.

18 "Belgian Cardinal Adds to Talk of Pope Resigning," *Associated Press*, October 20, 2000.

what they hope will happen, intending their predictions to help bring it about."[19]

"When prominent prelates openly speculate about the pope's retirement, it is for the purpose of making the idea more acceptable," says Hitchcock. "The fact that the two bishops have spoken publicly might also mean that the idea has been proposed to the pope and has been rejected, and that an attempt is now being made to mount public pressure for such an action, to discredit the Holy Father by suggesting that important prelates believe that he is no longer fit for office."[20]

* * *

For the shadowy force could not stay submerged; it ached to rise up. In January 2004, when the ailing Pope John Paul II still remained in office, the mafia's annual meeting at St. Gallen took place.

That same month, Danneels took up the old war against *Humanae Vitae.*

"Someone who is infected with the HIV virus, and decides to have sex with an uninfected person, has to protect his partner by using a condom," said Danneels, opening with a highly specific case. Soon, the mafia's Murphy-O'Connor echoed Danneels's position in the media.[21]

Then the unyielding Pope John Paul II died.

At the Brussels airport shortly before the funeral, cloaked in black, Danneels said the new pope would have to minister to the "needs for the future of the Church," including those of

19   James Hitchcock, "Thinking about the Papal Succession," Catholic Education Resource Center, January 2001, https://www.catholiceducation.org/en/culture/catholic-contributions/thinking-about-the-papal-succession.html.

20   Hitchcock, "Thinking about the Papal Succession."

21   John Walsh, "More Tea, Cardinal?" *The Independent*, October 22, 2011, https://www.independent.co.uk/news/uk/this-britain/more-tea-cardinal-554503.html.

"America Latina."[22] But when Ratzinger, the German, was elected pope instead of Bergoglio, the Latin American, Danneels could no longer hold in his emotions.

"This conclave tells us that the Church is not yet ready for a Latin American pope!" cried Danneels to the other cardinals, behind closed doors right after the election.[23]

When Pope Benedict invited all the cardinals to a spur-of-the-moment supper that night, Danneels, with a number of other cardinals, snubbed the new pope and skipped it. After riding in a car to the Belgian College, Danneels made it known to reporters that Benedict had not been his choice.

"No, we don't have to accept the pope's theology. It may change. I hope it does," said Danneels.[24]

Then, like other mafia members, he added a prophecy of Ratzinger's transformation.

"As pope, he will be a different man than he was as a cardinal," Danneels said.[25]

---

22 Associated Press, "Interview with Cardinal Danneels, Seen as Papal Contender," YouTube video, 1:30, July 21, 2015, https://www.youtube.com/watch?v=jHHE7GTB8cA.

23 Gerard O'Connell, *The Election of Pope Francis: An Inside Account of the Conclave that Changed History* (Maryknoll, NY: Orbis, 2019), 46, NOOK.

24 Robert Blair Kaiser, *A Church in Search of Itself: Benedict XVI and the Battle for the Future* (New York: Vintage, 2006), 219, Kindle.

25 Kaiser, *A Church in Search*, 219.

6

The Ante-Pope

Officially, it is said that the St. Gallen mafia disbanded soon after Benedict's election, its momentum dissipated and its purpose no longer clear.[1]

But as the mysterious cardinal of *Confession d'un Cardinal* named the subversive projects of Martini, Kasper, and Danneels, you felt the presence of an intelligence that was planning its next step.

In April 2006, St. Gallen's spirit peered from Martini's piercing blue eyes on the cover of the Italian magazine *L'Espresso*. There, the cardinal, dressed in the severity of black and red, launched what Sandro Magister calls "the first great act of opposition" to Benedict's pontificate from the Church's upper echelons.[2]

---

1   Edward Pentin, "Cardinal Danneels' Biographers Retract Comments on St. Gallen Group," *The National Catholic Register*, September 26, 2015, https://www.ncregister.com/blog/cardinal-danneels-biographers-retract-comments-on-st-gallen-group.

2   Sandro Magister, "When Does Life Begin? Cardinal Martini Replies," *L'Espresso*, April 24, 2006, https://chiesa.espresso.repubblica.it/articolo/51790%26eng%3Dy.html.

It came almost a year to the day of Benedict's first anniversary as pope—a bombshell interview on bioethics from Martini. When he was hailed as "the next pope" on the magazine covers of 1993, Martini had only hinted at changes in the Church. Now, he embraced the notion of moral "gray areas" in an interview that some claimed read "like the manifesto of an antipope."[3]

He said that life did not begin immediately with fertilization but rather sometime later. Martini urged the Church to move past "the rejection of every form of artificial fertilization."[4]

He said, "Certainly, in some situations the use of condoms can constitute a lesser evil." Then Martini flagged the situation of a spouse with AIDS.

He said, on abortion, "It is important to acknowledge that the pursuit of physical human life is not, in itself, the first and absolute principle." Then Martini spoke of what a "good thing" it was that "the law should contribute to reducing" clandestine abortions by providing for legal abortion.

"I maintain that respect must be granted to every person who, perhaps after much reflection and suffering, follows her own conscience even if she decides to do something that I do not feel I can approve of," Martini said of abortion. Later, he reiterated that the Church's task was not to dispense "prohibitions" but to "form consciences" and teach "discernment."

"So now the Trojan horse has been brought into the city," someone from the Congregation for the Doctrine of the Faith lamented.[5]

---

3   Sandro Magister, "Carlo Maria Martini's 'Day After,'" *L'Espresso*, April 28, 2006, http://chiesa.espresso.repubblica.it/articolo/53021bdc4.html.

4   Magister, "When Does Life Begin?" All subsequent quotations from Martini's interview are from this source.

5   Magister, "Martini's Day After."

A copy of *L'Espresso* lay on the table, Martini's strong face looking out from the cover.

* * *

Immediately after Martini's interview was published, it came to light that the Congregation for the Doctrine of the Faith was already studying a document on condoms—at the personal request of Benedict himself.

The secret commission, said Vatican experts, came specifically in response to the 2004 statements from Danneels and Murphy-O'Connor on condoms.

"Cardinal Murphy-O'Connor informed me after one visit to Rome that Cardinal Ratzinger had told him that 'we cannot have cardinals disagreeing about this.' Soon after came the news that the report had been commissioned from a group of eminent moral theologians," said Austen Ivereigh, Murphy-O'Connor's then press secretary.[6]

Benedict already had a long history of issuing negative answers on the question. In 1987, Ratzinger admonished the US bishops for trying to circumvent Rome on the issue of condoms.[7] In 2005, as Pope Benedict, he reaffirmed that "the traditional teaching of the Church has proven to be the only failsafe way to prevent the spread of HIV/AIDS."[8]

But now, one vaticanista wondered, was Martini renewing the media row over condoms to try to steer Benedict's

---

6 Austen Ivereigh, "AIDS, Condoms, and the Suppression of Theological Truth," *America Magazine*, February 11, 2010, https://www.americama gazine.org/content/all-things/aids-condoms-and-suppression-theologic al-truth.

7 Russell Chandler and John Dart, "Bishops' Panel Rejects Condoms in AIDS Battle," *The Los Angeles Times*, October 13, 1989, https://www .latimes.com/archives/la-xpm-1989-10-13-mn-149-story.html.

8 Magister, "When Does Life Begin?"

commission?[9] The commission's very existence had been draped in secrecy before Martini's bombshell interview.

Meanwhile, *The New York Times* wondered about Benedict's "capacity to surprise." It wondered if, like "Nixon in China," Benedict the "hard-liner" could, "without reversing church doctrine, more easily make" changes in praxis on condoms.[10]

"Only Nixon could go to China." It is a phrase that vaticanista John Allen Jr. echoes in his well-sourced book on the 2005 conclave. According to Allen, Ratzinger was elected in part because "some cardinals felt the Church was long overdue for some reforms that only someone of Ratzinger's stature and unquestioned orthodoxy could engineer."[11]

But in the summer of 2006, the pope summoned Martini to Castel Gandolfo.

There, says *The Tablet*, Benedict expressed his disappointment over Martini's "gray areas" interview.[12]

✳ ✳ ✳

In early 2007, Pope Benedict released *Sacramentum Caritatis*. It rejected the Kasper proposal for Communion for the divorced and civilly remarried, defended priestly celibacy, and called on politicians to defend marriage and human life.[13]

---

9   Robert Mickens, "Clarion Call on Condoms," *The Tablet*, April 29, 2006.

10   Ian Fisher, "Ideals Collide as Vatican Rethinks Condom Ban," *The New York Times*, May 2, 2005, https://www.nytimes.com/2006/05/02/world/europe/02pope.html.

11   John Allen Jr., *The Rise of Benedict XVI: The Inside Story of How the Pope Was Elected and Where He Will Take the Church* (New York: Doubleday, 2007), 118, NOOK.

12   Robert Mickens, "Letter from Rome," *The Tablet*, April 16, 2011.

13   Benedict XVI, *Sacramentum Caritatis*, Vatican website, https://www.vatican.va/content/benedict-xvi/en/apost_exhortations/documents/hf_ben-xvi_exh_20070222_sacramentum-caritatis.html.

Meanwhile, somewhere in Jerusalem in 2007, Martini stayed up late into the night dreaming of revolution, generating a new book called *Night Conversations with Cardinal Martini*.

"Much of what we discussed at these [St. Gallen] meetings"—says one mafia member—"Martini worked into the book."[14]

In *Night Conversations*, Martini eerily called himself an "ante-pope, a precursor and preparer for the Holy Father." This notion was, says author Antonio Socci, a clever wordplay for evading accusations of being an "antipope."[15]

The name sought to answer an old accusation: how could a Jesuit justify dissent, given his special fourth vow of obedience to the pope? As Socci and vaticanista Robert Moynihan point out, Karl Rahner, SJ, had an alleged solution.[16]

As one Jesuit explained in the 1990s: "Rahner was able to exhort his fellow Jesuits: 'You must remain loyal to the papacy in theology and in practice, because that is part of your heritage to a special degree, but because the actual form of the papacy remains subject, in the future too, to an historical process of change, your theology and ecclesiastical law has above all to serve the papacy as it will be in the future.' See the move? Our current Jesuits are all loyal to the papacy, but to the future papacy."[17]

---

14   See Maike Hickson, "Evidence Pope Follows Blueprint to Change Church by Dissident Cardinal who Led St. Gallen 'Mafia,'" LifeSiteNews, March 29, 2019, https://www.lifesitenews.com/blogs/evidence-pope-follows -blueprint-to-change-church-by-dissident-cardinal-who-led-st.-gallen- mafia.

15   Antonio Socci, *Non è Francesco. La Chiesa Nella Grande Tempesta* (Milan: Mondadori, 2015), 240–246.

16   Robert Moynihan, "Letter #52, 2019: The Jesuits, Part #2," *Inside the Vatican*, October 5, 2019, https://insidethevatican.com/news/newsflash /letter-52-2019-the-jesuits-part-2/; Socci, *Non è Francesco*, 240–246.

17   Paul Shaughnessy, S.J., "Are the Jesuits Catholic?" *The Weekly Standard*,

So dissent was only a manifestation of being ahead of the times, of anticipating some once and future pope.

But this dream of a revolutionary pope was more than just a Jesuit idea, Socci says. Socci traces the dream back to Modernism—a heretical movement that believes, perhaps most essentially, that truth is not immutable. Modernists—to borrow a description from Paul Kengor—were "moral relativists, cultural relativists, human-nature redefiners, fundamental transformers. Their enemies were absolutes, religion, tradition. . . . They believe that truths and values can and do evolve, change, *progress* along with or relative to society, culture, norms, history."[18]

And according to Socci, the Modernists had long ago set their sights on the papacy itself. As Socci notes, the early twentieth-century "father of Modernism," Ernesto Buoniauti, had a disturbing prophecy of a revolution from above. Change would come not from outside the Church but from within, from the Church's highest echelons.[19]

Now, the dream of presaging a revolutionary pope grew within Martini. In *Night Conversations*, Martini thought out loud: "Whatever I begin, others will have to carry on."[20] He recalled how the prophet Joel had foretold old men who would dream dreams—and a middle generation of visionaries who would carry those dreams out. Martini said he no longer had

---

June 3, 2002, https://www.washingtonexaminer.com/weekly-standard /are-the-jesuits-catholic.

18   Paul Kengor, *The Devil and Karl Marx* (Gastonia, NC: TAN Books, 2020), 394, Kindle.

19   Socci, *Non è Francesco*, 241.

20   Carlo Maria Martini and Georg Sporschill, *Night Conversations with Cardinal Martini*, trans. Lorna Henry (New York: Paulist Press, 2012), 30, NOOK.

dreams for the Church; he was actively praying for their fulfill-ment, moving from dreaming to preparing the way.[21]

He was the ante-pope.

* * *

"There is certainly a tendency to retreat from the Council," Martini continued in *Night Conversations*.[22]

Then he spoke of how theologians such as Rahner had still carried Vatican II "forward."[23] And there it was, resonant and clear: the echo of Rahner's *The Shape of the Church to Come*, which had envisioned change on Communion for the divorced and civilly remarried, the ordination of married men and women, and more.

Speaking of celibacy in *Night Conversations*, Martini said that the possibility of ordaining proven married men—*viri probati*—was "worth discussing."[24] Speaking of women in the Church, Martini mentioned "deaconesses" as well as his words of encouragement to the primate of the Church of England during the firestorm surrounding women's ordination.[25]

"I tried to give him courage to take a risk that could also help us treat women more fairly and understand how things might develop further," Martini said. "We should not be unhappy that the Protestant and Anglican Churches ordain women and are thereby introducing something important into the arena of wider ecumenism."[26]

21 Martini and Sporschill, *Night Conversations with Cardinal Martini*, 47–49.
22 Martini and Sporschill, *Night Conversations with Cardinal Martini*, 79.
23 Martini and Sporschill, *Night Conversations with Cardinal Martini*, 79.
24 Martini and Sporschill, *Night Conversations with Cardinal Martini*, 78.
25 Martini and Sporschill, *Night Conversations with Cardinal Martini*, 84.
26 Martini and Sporschill, *Night Conversations with Cardinal Martini*, 84.

Then Martini lamented the "major damage" that Paul VI's *Humanae Vitae* had caused. He accused Paul VI of being deceptive about contraception, of concealing the truth about its moral status. As a result, moralists "have to clarify where sin begins, especially where there is a greater duty than the transmission of life."[27]

"In the Vatican discussions have been taking place about the use of condoms, not least because the pope is deeply concerned about the AIDS epidemic," Martini said. He was resurrecting an old issue from the "gray areas" interview that had disappointed Benedict. Then Martini admitted that all the talk about spouses with AIDS was aimed at a greater change. "Even if condoms were allowed for HIV-infected couples as a 'lesser evil,' that is probably not enough," he said.[28]

Thus, on everything he could, he prepared.

Then the ante-pope waited.

✳ ✳ ✳

Shortly after the Italian publication of *Night Conversations*, Pope Benedict implicitly responded to Martini.

Benedict was on a 2009 trip to Africa. A French reporter said, "The position of the Catholic Church on the way to fight [AIDS] is often considered unrealistic and ineffective. Will you address this theme during the journey?"

All the media questions were selected beforehand, giving Benedict time to consider his answer.

"I think that the most efficient, most truly present player in the fight against AIDS is the Catholic Church herself," the pope said. "If there is no human dimension, if Africans do not help [by responsible behavior], the problem [of AIDS] cannot

---

27   Martini and Sporschill, *Night Conversations with Cardinal Martini*, 70–71.
28   Martini and Sporschill, *Night Conversations with Cardinal Martini*, 73.

be overcome by the distribution of prophylactics: on the contrary, they increase it."[29]

And with that, the fires leapt from the Trojan horse.

"Unprecedented condemnations" of Benedict filled major papers; the Belgian parliament pursued a resolution to censure the pope.[30]

European political officials condemned Benedict's position; the Spanish government vowed to send Africa one million condoms.[31]

And until he returned home, Benedict was kept in the dark about the blaze's scorching immensity.

More and more, the pope seemed to be trapped in a "terrible solitude."[32]

29   "Interview of the Holy Father Benedict XVI During the Flight to Africa,"
      Vatican website, March 17, 2009, http://www.vatican.va/content/bened
      ict-xvi/en/speeches/2009/march/documents/hf_ben-xvi_spe_20090317
      _africa-interview.html.

30   Philip Pullella, "Vatican Deplores Belgian Censure of Pope on Con-
      doms," *Reuters*, April 17, 2009, https://www.reuters.com/article/us-pope
      -condoms-belgium-idUSTRE53G2WE20090417.

31   Hilary White, "World Leaders, Condom-Promoting Forces Attack Pope
      Over Condom AIDS Remarks," LifeSiteNews, March 19, 2009, https://
      www.lifesitenews.com/news/world-leaders-condom-promoting-forces
      -attack-pope-over-condom-aids-remarks.

32   Nicolas Diat, *L'Homme Qui Ne Voulait Pas Être Pape: Histoire Secrète d'un
      Règne* (Paris: Albin Michel, 2014), 348.

7

Fire

B ack in 2005, the mysterious cardinal of *Confession d'un Cardinal* had already explained what Benedict was supposed to do.

The mysterious cardinal once said that the very act of creating a commission on a topic told the world that the Church was open to change.[1] And the way he saw it, Ratzinger's own 1996 book *Salt of the Earth* had pried the debate over contraception wide open.[2]

"The question remains whether you can reproach someone, say a couple who already have several children, for not having a positive attitude toward children," said Peter Seewald in the book.

"No, of course not, and that shouldn't happen, either," Ratzinger said.

"But must these people nevertheless have the idea that they are living in some sort of sin if they . . ."

---

1   Olivier Le Gendre, *Confession d'un Cardinal* (Paris: JC Lattès, 2007), 99, NOOK.

2   Le Gendre, *Confession d'un Cardinal*, 31–32.

"I would say that those are questions that ought to be discussed with one's spiritual director, with one's priest, because they can't be projected into the abstract," Ratzinger said.[3]

For the mysterious cardinal of *Confession d'un Cardinal*, that statement amounted to a confession that exceptions to the contraception ban could be given.[4]

But—interrupted his French interlocutor—the mysterious cardinal had been wrong: nothing had come of Ratzinger's statements.

But then the mysterious cardinal asked, who could swear that there were not "hidden events," that nothing was "being prepared"? The mysterious cardinal and his collaborators did not like to publicize their work until it was successful. Who could say for certain that Pope Benedict would not elevate his 1996 opinion into a papal act?[5]

Another time, the mysterious cardinal said that, with time, Benedict's view of the Church would "broaden." At first, Benedict would make "clumsy," "abrupt" declarations. But then, confronted with "pained and shocked reactions," Benedict would "humanize" his language, worrying less about professing truth and more about respecting others' spiritual paths. He would, in short, act less like a theologian and more like a "pastor."[6]

Benedict was "already listening to us," the mysterious cardinal said. Even if the pope could not "really hear us yet," he was listening.[7]

3   Joseph Ratzinger and Peter Seewald, *Salt of the Earth: The Church at the End of the Millennium* (San Francisco: Ignatius Press, 2017), 202, Kindle.

4   Le Gendre, *Confession d'un Cardinal*, 31–32.

5   Le Gendre, *Confession d'un Cardinal*, 32.

6   Le Gendre, *Confession d'un Cardinal*, 308.

7   Le Gendre, *Confession d'un Cardinal*, 309.

Back in 1999, a mysterious group called the Millenari had said something relevant to this question of "listening."

Claiming that Silvestrini was the "ring leader" of a dominant "gang" in the Vatican, the Millenari feared that the next pope—even if he was not the kind to be manipulated by revolutionary forces—would still have to "compromise" on Church matters since "all of the important positions in the Curia" were held by the group.[8]

* * *

Time passed. In 2010, two Vatican experts released an Italian book detailing the "attack on Ratzinger."

Attacco a Ratzinger spoke of a war against Benedict from three primary actors—summarized by another vaticanista, Sandro Magister.

First, said Magister, came the worldly, external enemies of the Church.

Second came the Modernists lurking within the Church.

Third came the Curial members who consciously or unconsciously hurt and thwarted the pope.[9]

"It does not appear that these three fronts are commanded by the same general," said Magister. "But this does not mean that a unifying reason cannot be sought that would explain such bitter and constant attacks."[10]

Then Magister sketched Pope Benedict's plan: Restoring the ancient liturgy through *Summorum Pontificum*. Upholding

---

8   The Millenari, *Shroud of Secrecy: The Story of Corruption Within the Vatican*, trans. Ian Martin (Toronto: Key Porter Books, 2000), 92–93. This clan from Emilia Romagna "has the most influence and ability to secure the candidature of the next Pope," said the Millenari in 1999.

9   Sandro Magister, "'Why They Are Attacking Me.' Autobiography of a Pontificate," September 3, 2010, *L'Espresso*, https://chiesa.espresso. repubblica.it/articolo/1344604bdc4.html.

10 Magister, "Why They Are Attacking Me."

priestly celibacy against the Modernists. Defending the family and human life against the dictatorship of relativism.

"There is a mysterious lucidity of vision that unifies the attacks on the current pontificate," said Magister. "As if an 'invisible hand' were at work in them, hidden from their own authors. A hand, a mind that glimpses Benedict XVI's basic plan, and therefore does all it can to oppose it."[11]

Another reviewer of *Attacco a Ratzinger* spoke of a complex galaxy of fellow travelers united in seeing the pope as the "principal obstacle" to a "universal dictatorship of relativism."[12]

But what did this eerie, grappling intelligence look like? *Attacco a Ratzinger* offered one still shot of it, detailing an unsettling memory from an anonymous cardinal.

Years later, this cardinal could still remember watching a powerful Italian cardinal of the Curia the day after Benedict's election. "Two or three years, he will only last two or three years," the powerful Italian had said, making a gesture of his hands, as if to diminish Benedict. For the new pope was supposed to be a transitional figure—passing quickly, without leaving a legacy.[13]

Then the anonymous cardinal who had watched the powerful Italian remembered something Ratzinger had said in the Sistine Chapel just after his election. The new pope told the cardinals he had chosen his name in part because Benedict XV had had a short pontificate, one dedicated to peace.

Recalling that old memory now, the anonymous cardinal could see why the attacks had "multiplied." Benedict's pontificate

11   Magister, "Why They Are Attacking Me."

12   Massimo Introvigne, "I Tre Nemici del Papa. 'Attacco a Ratzinger' di Paolo Rodari e Andrea Tornielli," CESNUR website, 2010, https://www .cesnur.org/2010/mi-ratzinger.html.

13   Paolo Rodari and Andrea Tornielli, *Attacco a Ratzinger: Accuse e Scandali, Profezie e Complotti Contro Benedetto XVI* (Milan: Mondadori, 2010), 5–6.

had not passed quickly enough. Now, "attacks of every kind" besieged Benedict, and the anonymous cardinal thought of how alone, "objectively," the pope really was.[14]

* * *

He was alone, but still he tried to pursue his plan. On June 19, 2009—the feast of the Sacred Heart—Pope Benedict proclaimed a Year for Priests.

"The Lord has drawn us to his heart—*suscepit nos Dominus in sinum et cor suum*," he said, quoting the day's antiphon. Then, as if imparting a precious secret, Benedict spoke of cooperating with a plan by which "Jesus gradually becomes the Heart of human hearts, beginning with those called to be closest to him: namely his priests."[15]

It was beautiful. It was hard not to think of seven-year-old Ratzinger, who once wrote the Christ child a Christmas letter asking for a missal, priestly clothes, and an image of the Sacred Heart.[16]

And it was hard not to think of the time, years later, when Ratzinger was a young German forced into military service during World War II and there were orders to shoot deserters on the spot.

One day, Ratzinger decided to just leave. He took a little-known back road when suddenly, two soldiers met him by a railroad underpass. All around Ratzinger's home village, SS men had been hanging deserters from trees.[17]

14 Rodari and Tornielli, *Attacco a Ratzinger*, 5–6.
15 "Homily of His Holiness Benedict XVI," Vatican website, June 19, 2009, http://www.vatican.va/content/benedict-xvi/en/homilies/2009/docume nts/hf_ben-xvi_hom_20090619_anno-sac.html.
16 "Pope's Childhood Letter to Baby Jesus Shows His Faith," *Catholic News Agency*, December 21, 2012, https://www.catholicnewsagency.com/news /popes-childhood-letter-to-baby-jesus-shows-his-faith.
17 Joseph Ratzinger, *Milestones: Memoirs* (San Francisco: Ignatius Press,

Providentially, the soldiers passed over Ratzinger. Later, Ratzinger got his official certificate of release, arriving in his hometown before sunset. "I heard praying and singing coming from the church," he later recalled. "It was the evening of the Feast of the Sacred Heart of Jesus."[18]

But the 2009–2010 Year for Priests, inaugurated on another feast of the Sacred Heart, did not turn out as Benedict had planned. It soon metamorphosed into an *annus horribilis*, a year of disaster, during which the most terrible sins of clergy came to light.

In his 2010 book *Light of the World* with Peter Seewald, Benedict spoke of something like "the crater of a volcano, out of which suddenly a tremendous cloud of filth came, darkening and soiling everything, so that above all the priesthood suddenly seemed to be a place of shame."[19]

"One might think that the devil could not stand the Year for Priests and therefore threw this filth in our faces," Benedict said.[20]

But even if so many of these cases were old—Seewald finally said to Benedict—they "now burden your pontificate in particular. Have you thought of resigning?"

"When the danger is great one must not run away," said the pope. He spoke of how "now" was "not the time to resign," but how one could resign "at a peaceful moment."[21]

"If a pope clearly realizes that he is no longer physically, psychologically, and spiritually capable of handling the duties

1998), 36, Kindle.

18   Ratzinger, *Milestones*, 38–39.
19   Benedict XVI and Peter Seewald, *Light of the World: The Pope, the Church, and the Signs of the Times*, trans. Michael Miller and Adrian Walker (San Francisco: Ignatius, 2010), 34, Kindle.
20   Benedict XVI and Seewald, *Light of the World*, 43.
21   Benedict XVI and Seewald, *Light of the World*, 39.

of his office, then he has a right and, under some circumstances, also an obligation to resign," Benedict ultimately said.[22]

❊ ❊ ❊

Benedict's 2010 dialogue with Seewald continued. The journalist wanted to know more about the firestorm surrounding the pope's remarks on condoms during his 2009 trip to Africa.

"[I] merely said, and this is what caused such great offense, that we cannot solve the problem [of AIDS] by distributing condoms," said Benedict.[23]

"There may be a basis in the case of some individuals, as perhaps when a male prostitute uses a condom, where this can be a first step in the direction of a moralization, a first assumption of responsibility, on the way toward recovering an awareness that not everything is allowed and that one cannot do whatever one wants," Benedict continued, ambiguously. Then he added, "But it is not really the way to deal with the evil of HIV infection."[24]

"Are you saying, then, that the Catholic Church is actually not opposed in principle to the use of condoms?" Seewald asked.

"She of course does not regard it as a real or moral solution, but, in this or that case, there can be nonetheless, in the intention of reducing the risk of infection, a first step in a movement toward a different way, a more human way, of living sexuality," said Benedict.[25]

Before the publication embargo was lifted, the Vatican's semi-official newspaper leaked the excerpts on AIDS and

22 Benedict XVI and Seewald, *Light of the World*, 39.
23 Benedict XVI and Seewald, *Light of the World*, 112.
24 Benedict XVI and Seewald, *Light of the World*, 112.
25 Benedict XVI and Seewald, *Light of the World*, 112.

prostitutes. Certain key words were mysteriously mistranslated, insinuating a clear "justification" for condoms.[26]

"Pope Says Condoms Are Cool 'In Certain Cases,'" cried *The Village Voice*. "Pope: Condoms OK—for Male Prostitutes," said *The New York Post*.

Benedict's pontificate was on fire again.

The Congregation for the Doctrine of the Faith quickly explained that the pope's words did "not signify a change" in moral teaching or pastoral practice.[27] Kenya's episcopal conference said that Benedict spoke merely of "subjective moral journeying"—and that to maintain that condoms were now justified "would be an offense to the pope's intelligence and a gratuitous manipulation of his words."[28]

Christine Vollmer of the Pontifical Academy for Life said that the pope was "betrayed by the premature presentation" of *Light of the World*'s contents. "The fact that those paragraphs were also translated poorly and treacherously reinforces this betrayal," she said.[29]

But in late 2010, the mysterious cardinal of *Confession d'un Cardinal* was watching the fire too.

* * *

The mysterious cardinal had already insinuated the need for a more permissive stance on condoms in 2005, in relation to

---

26   For more on the mistranslation issue, see Sandro Magister, "Friendly Fire on Benedict XVI. And a Condom's to Blame," *L'Espresso*, December 1, 2010, http://chiesa.espresso.repubblica.it/articolo/1345793bdc4. html?eng=y.

27   John Allen Jr., "Condoms Not a 'Lesser Evil,' Vatican Insists," *The National Catholic Reporter*, December 21, 2010, https://www.ncronline.org/blo gs/ncr-today/condoms-not-lesser-evil-vatican-insists.

28   Sandro Magister, "Church and Condoms. The 'No' of the Diehards," *L'Espresso*, December 4, 2010, http://chiesa.espresso.repubblica.it/artico lo/1345841bdc4.html.

29   Magister, "Church and Condoms."

Southeast Asian prostitutes.[30] Now, he presented the situation with Benedict as a specimen of "hypocrisy."

The semi-official newspaper's violation of the publication embargo had mobilized the rigorists to say that the excerpts were decontextualized and mistranslated, he said. Meanwhile, as a hermeneutical war raged over the interview's proper interpretation, everyone had to separate, cleanly, the private opinions of Ratzinger from the papal acts of Benedict. It was, in the mysterious cardinal's mind, hypocrisy to bifurcate the pope in this way.[31]

And as he spoke in his 2011 book *L'Espérance du Cardinal*, the mysterious cardinal talked over and over again of fire. The word appeared some twenty-three times in his book, naming the conflagrations from the sexual abuse scandal and more.

"The air was more and more filled with smoke and the smell of fire," Ratzinger had said of his experience in Germany during World War II.[32] But now, said one vaticanista, "the tragedy of Benedict's papacy" was that the pope's own schoolhouse was "burning down."[33]

30 Le Gendre, *Confession d'un Cardinal*, 274–275.
31 Olivier Le Gendre, *L'Espérance du Cardinal* (Paris: JC Lattès, 2011), 227, NOOK.
32 Ratzinger, *Milestones*, 32.
33 John Allen Jr., "'Attack on Ratzinger': Italian Book Assesses Benedict's Papacy," *The National Catholic Reporter*, August 27, 2010, https://www.ncronline.org/blogs/all-things-catholic/attack-ratzinger-italian-book-assesses-benedicts-papacy.

8

No Country for Old Men

When a vaticanista friend saw him in February 2011, a new light shone from Martini's eyes.

Outside, a heatless sun illuminated the cold pine trees by Gallarate, the Italian Jesuit residence that had become Martini's home after the old cardinal repeatedly fell in Jerusalem. Inside, Martini sat in a white armchair next to the sunlight. His voice faltered from Parkinson's, but his eyes were brilliant. Martini explained, among other things, that his eyes shone the need for "openness" on Communion for the divorced and civilly remarried.[1]

Two months later, Martini sent a letter to Pope Benedict. Martini feared that a hard line on doctrine would distance the Church from listening. Every day, he received messages from people of every rank stressing this point.[2]

Martini wanted to tell Benedict.

And so he wrote what biographer Marco Garzonio calls an "affectionate" letter to the pope.[3] Sexual ethics, Communion for

---

1   Aldo Maria Valli, *Storia di un Uomo: Ritratto di Carlo Maria Martini* (Milan: Ancora, 2011), loc. 2935 of 3334, Kindle.

2   Valli, *Storia di un Uomo*, loc. 395 of 3334.

3   Marco Garzonio, "Perché Martini Avrebbe Apprezzato L'Addio," *Corriere*

the divorced and civilly remarried, the relationship between the Church and political power—these were the great themes of Martini's letter.[4]

Martini was sure that he would receive no answer.

But then, with simplicity, it came—a reply from Benedict inviting Martini to visit on April 9, 2011 at 11:00 a.m.[5]

Martini readied himself.

He had first encountered Ratzinger's work in the 1960s. Later, after Martini and Ratzinger met at the 1980 synod on the family, Ratzinger sought out Martini for work with the Congregation for the Doctrine of the Faith. In a glowing 1995 tribute, Ratzinger spoke of how Martini, despite all his differences, complemented him.[6]

And there it was—Benedict's generosity, his largeness of heart, the part of him that stood by old friends and collaborators with uncomplicated loyalty. The part of him that, with disarming simplicity, praised Martini to a group of young people—just two weeks before the mafia leader released the 2006 bioethics manifesto that Sandro Magister called the highest-level attack on Benedict to date.[7]

The night before he met with Benedict in April 2011, Martini could not sleep.[8]

He had been used to speaking "completely freely with Cardinal Ratzinger over a ten-year period" in the Congregation

della Sera, February 13, 2013.

4   Valli, *Storia di un Uomo*, loc. 395 of 3334.

5   Damiano Modena, *Carlo Maria Martini: Il Silenzio della Parola* (Milan: San Paolo, 2013), loc. 600 of 1190, Kindle.

6   Valli, *Storia di un Uomo*, loc. 324 of 3334.

7   Sandro Magister, "When Does Life Begin? Cardinal Martini Replies," *L'Espresso*, April 24, 2006, https://chiesa.espresso.repubblica.it/ articolo/51790%26eng%3Dy.html.

8   Modena, *Carlo Maria Martini*, loc. 600 of 1190.

for the Doctrine of the Faith.[9] Now, Parkinson's had stripped Martini's strong Italian voice down to something scrawny, raspy.

Before his meeting with the pope, Martini and his priest-secretary went over some vocal drills in the Vatican's halls. The door of the pope's library opened. Slowly, with open arms, Martini walked toward the pope. The two men embraced and sat down. Martini made some preliminary pleasantries, stammering—until his voice went out.[10]

Martini took out a prepared note for the pope.

In 2013, Martini's priest-secretary published the note. The text is full of elisions, but there is a reference to a prior letter to Benedict on "grave and secret things." Then there is hopeful talk of some "sign" that would give "audacity."[11]

Once, Martini had described the meeting this way: he had said things that the pope's collaborators did not say. Very hard things.[12]

* * *

Time passed. One hot day in June 2012, Martini met Benedict for the last time, at the World Meeting of Families in Milan.

It was shortly after the pope's butler had been arrested in the Vatileaks scandal under suspicion of leaking sensitive documents.

According to a cardinal who was with Benedict in Milan, the pope suffered unspeakably.[13]

---

9   Carlo Maria Martini and Georg Sporschill, *Night Conversations with Cardinal Martini*, trans. Lorna Henry (New York: Paulist Press, 2012), 33, NOOK.

10 Modena, *Carlo Maria Martini*, loc. 608 of 1190

11 Modena, *Carlo Maria Martini*, loc. 608 of 1190

12 Marco Garzonio, *Il Profeta: Vita di Carlo Maria Martini* (Milan: Mondadori, 2012), 453.

13 Nicolas Diat, *L'Homme Qui Ne Voulait Pas Être Pape: Histoire Secrète d'un Règne* (Paris: Albin Michel, 2014), 274.

When it was time to meet with Martini, Benedict walked forward and offered his hand. Martini, looking very frail and aged, took the hand to draw the pontiff closer, then clasped Benedict's upper arm tightly.[14] The embrace, as Martini's priest-secretary recalls, was so close as to leave the two men's heads resting on each other's shoulders.[15]

For ten minutes, they met.

Later that summer, journalist and atheist Eugenio Scalfari visited Martini for the last time. The cardinal was still lucid in mind but could only express himself with soundless movements of the lips, translated by a young priest. Like an old dreamer, Martini kept speaking of how the Church was going to be modernized. Then he specifically explained the main positions that he shared fully with Bergoglio.[16]

Bergoglio. According to Scalfari, Martini was by this point "very fond" of the Argentinian.[17] By 2009, Martini was even referencing Bergoglio in his work.[18] Somehow, the differences separating Bergoglio and Martini at the 2005 conclave had dissipated.

A few weeks after Scalfari's visit, Martini's condition deteriorated. On August 31, 2012, a powerful wind gusted outside,

---

14   AvvenireNEI, "Papa Benedetto e il Cardinal Martini," YouTube video, 1:07, September 5, 2012, https://www.youtube.com/watch?v=4VBQRQ 9kPIs.

15   Modena, *Carlo Maria Martini*, loc. 632 of 1190.

16   Eugenio Scalfari, "Quel Rivoluzionario del Mio Amico Francesco," *La Repubblica*, November 2, 2019, https://rep.repubblica.it/pwa/editoriale /2019/11/02/news/quel_rivoluzionario_del_mio_amico_francesco-240 105313/.

17   Scalfari, "Quel Rivoluzionario."

18   Carlo Maria Martini, *Qualcosa di Cosi Personale: Meditazioni sulla Preghiera* (Milan: Mondadori, 2009), 131.

shaking the trees in the middle of the day. A few hours later, Martini died.[19]

That was no country for old men.

But the next day, with the publication of his last testament, Martini's spirit rose up like a revenant, speaking from beyond the grave.[20]

The old cardinal said that the Church was "tired," that her rites and garments were "pompous." "But do these things express what we are today?"

He said that the Church should admit her "errors," and "undertake a radical journey of change, beginning with the pope and the bishops." This "journey of conversion" should involve "questions about sexuality and about all of the topics that involve the body."

He spoke of the autonomy of conscience, said that "neither the clergy nor ecclesial law could replace the interiority of man." "All of the external rules, the laws, the dogmas are given to us in order to clarify the internal voice and for the discernment of spirits."

He said, "Do we take the sacraments to men who require new strength? I am thinking of all of the divorced and of remarried couples, of expanded families. . . . The question of whether the divorced can receive communion must be turned around. How can the Church, with the power of the sacraments, come to the aid of those who have complex family situations?"

Then he said, "The Church is 200 years behind. Why in the world does it not rouse itself? Are we afraid? Fear instead of courage?"

---

19   Valli, *Storia di un Uomo*, loc. 3018 of 3334.

20   Sandro Magister, "After Martini, the Fight Over His Spiritual Testament," *L'Espresso*, September 6, 2012, http://chiesa.espresso.repubblica.it/artico lo/1350318bdc4.html?eng=y. All subsequent quotations of Martini's last testament are from this source.

"I see in the Church of today so much ash on top of the coals that I am often assailed by a sense of powerlessness," he sighed, invoking an image from Fr. Karl Rahner, SJ. "How can the coals be freed from the ashes so as to reinvigorate the flame of love?"

As Austen Ivereigh notes, Bergoglio could soon be heard quoting Martini, telling the coals to burn beneath the ashes of a Church that kept Jesus tied up in the sacristy.[21]

* * *

Around that same month—August 2012—a rumor that Pope Benedict was planning to resign crept through the Vatican.

You can hear a hint of Benedict's plan in Peter Seewald's August 2012 interview with the pope.

What more could we expect from this pontificate? Seewald wondered.

"From me? Not much," said Benedict. "I am an old man and the strength stops. I think what I have done is enough." Asked then if he would abdicate, Benedict said, "That depends on how much my physical strength will be necessary for me."[22]

All of Benedict's life—Seewald once said—could be seen as a "struggle for survival." "As a small child, when he had a narrow escape from death in surviving diptheria. Also in a second brush with death, when he nearly drowned in a pond. . . . In the war and the situation at the end of the war, when he survived not just blood poisoning, but also his desertion. And most of all, during the many years he was a persona non grata as the wicked *Panzerkardinal*."[23]

---

21   Austen Ivereigh, *The Great Reformer: Francis and the Making of a Radical Pope* (New York: Henry Holt & Co., 2014), 345–346, Kindle.

22   Edward Pentin, "Pope Benedict's Decision: Truth vs. Conjecture," *Edward Pentin* (blog), February 19, 2013, https://edwardpentin.co.uk/477/.

23   Peter Seewald, *Benedict XVI: An Intimate Portrait*, trans. Henry Taylor

Ultimately, Seewald saw that "there is something in Ratzinger that is like glass, something fragile." Something delicate, "like his tiny handwriting"—something shy, like the air of a schoolboy. Something that made him pull in his shoulders in a group of people and hold his briefcase up "like a shield." Something that made him become "narrow and little, as if he might break."[24]

In early 2012, amidst a trip to Mexico and Cuba, Benedict had fallen, striking his head on a bathroom sink. Vatican experts said the accident shook him, touching longtime fears of growing old while being pope.[25]

As early as 1978, Ratzinger had spoken of how Pope Paul VI had "struggled intensely with the notion of retiring." "We can imagine how heavily it must burden the mind . . . no longer to have a private moment," said Ratzinger then. "To be riveted to the end, while one's body gives out, to a task that demands, day after day, the full and vigorous exercise of all a man's strength."[26]

"The idea, almost haunting, of the fatigue of being pope as old age encroaches accompanied Benedict constantly," says Marco Politi. "At no time did Joseph Ratzinger desire the papacy. . . . Cardinal Poupard, an elector in 2005, recalls that 'as the decisive votes were counted in the conclave, Ratzinger had a despondent smile.'"[27]

It was despondent presumably because, as Ratzinger made clear in his 1998 memoir, as a bishop he felt like St. Corbinian's

and Anne Englund Nash (San Francisco: Ignatius, 2008), 54–55.

24 Seewald, *Benedict XVI: An Intimate Portrait*, 56.

25 Paul Vallely, *Pope Francis: The Struggle for the Soul of Catholicism* (London: Bloomsbury, 2015), loc. 704 of 11236, Kindle.

26 Quoted in Marco Politi, *Pope Francis Among the Wolves: The Inside Story of a Revolution* (New York: Columbia University Press, 2014), 23, Kindle.

27 Politi, *Pope Francis Among the Wolves*, 23.

bear, that mysterious figure which had inspired one of his episcopal symbols.

"The story has it that, on the way to Rome, a bear tore the
saint's horse to pieces," said Ratzinger. "Then Corbinian repri-
manded the bear sternly for its crime and as punishment loaded
on it the pack that the horse had been carrying. The bear had to
haul the pack all the way to Rome, and only there was it released
by the saint."[28]

The bear's weight reminded Ratzinger of St. Augustine: "he
had chosen the life of a scholar, but God had chosen to make
him into a 'draft animal.'" A scholar himself, Ratzinger then
spoke of how the Psalms helped Augustine "avoid all bitterness,"
but the ache in Ratzinger's voice remained.[29]

"It is said of Corbinian that, once in Rome, he again released
the bear to its freedom," said Ratzinger. "In the meantime I have
carried my load to Rome and have been now wandering the
streets of the Eternal City for a long time. I do not know when
I will be released."[30]

In his 2010 interview with Seewald, Benedict had said that
one must never run away when the danger is great.[31] Two years
later, in December 2012, the pope pardoned the butler at the
center of the Vatileaks scandal. As Benedict would later put it,
"calm had returned to this situation."[32] Around January 2013,

28   Joseph Ratzinger, *Milestones: Memoirs* (San Francisco: Ignatius Press,
     1998), 154, Kindle.
29   Ratzinger, *Milestones*, 154–155.
30   Ratzinger, *Milestones*, 155.
31   Benedict XVI and Peter Seewald, *Light of the World: The Pope, the Church,
     and the Signs of the Times*, trans. Michael Miller and Adrian Walker (San
     Francisco: Ignatius Press, 2010), 39, Kindle.
32   Benedict XVI and Peter Seewald, *Last Testament: In His Own Words*,
     trans. Jacob Phillips (London: Bloomsbury, 2016), 23, Kindle.

Benedict overcame any remaining hesitations and surrendered to the plan in his mind.[33]

* * *

On February 11, 2013, he announced it to the world.

"After having repeatedly examined my conscience before God, I have come to the certainty that my strengths, due to an advanced age, are no longer suited to an adequate exercise of the Petrine ministry," the pope said, reading his letter in Latin.[34] And with that, the hands that had once swung up in exhilaration over his 2005 election now clutched a piece of paper with apparent detachment.

Later, Benedict would seek to banish doubts about his resignation's integrity. Regarding whether his resignation was coerced, he said, "No one demanded it of me during my time as pope. No one." Regarding whether he resigned in response to the Vatileaks affair, Benedict said, "No, that is not right, not at all." Regarding blackmail, he said, "No one has tried to blackmail me." "On the contrary," he said, "the moment had—thanks be to God—a sense of having overcome the difficulties and a mood of peace. A mood in which one really could confidently pass the reins over to the next person."[35]

Later, Politi would argue that by resigning, Benedict had wanted "to sweep the board clear," to "reboot" the Vatican, to "trigger" the automatic resignation of key officials in the Church's broken government. Benedict, Politi and others would

---

33   Diat, *L'Homme*, 44.
34   "Declaratio," Vatican website, February 10, 2013, http://www.vatican
     .va/content/benedict-xvi/en/speeches/2013/february/documents/hf_
     ben-xvi_spe_20130211_declaratio.html.
35   Benedict XVI and Seewald, *Last Testament*, 26, 23.

suggest, wanted a conclave to choose Cardinal Angelo Scola for the job of reform.[36]

Later, a cardinal would say that Benedict had resigned because of a body broken with fatigue. It was a "miracle" that Benedict had not departed this world when "attacks" had left the old pope at the edge of Infinity.[37]

Later, vaticanista Edward Pentin would likewise describe Benedict's frailty and say the pope probably felt he only had a few months or years left to live. "I think he genuinely thought [resigning] was the right thing to do and that he felt he could not continue physically to [be pope]," said Pentin. At the same time, Pentin added, some decades earlier Ratzinger had touched on the issue of a pope emeritus, so perhaps he felt he could be a "trailblazer for resigning popes."[38]

Later, German Cardinal Walter Brandmüller lamented that Benedict "had no idea what would happen" when he created, *ex nihilo*, the office of pope emeritus for himself. The cardinal would argue that Celestine V, the last pontiff to abdicate, had at least "consulted the cardinals before he resigned"—while Pope Benedict made his choice "practically alone," evincing "disdain" for the cardinals.[39]

Later, Benedict's longtime personal secretary, Archbishop Georg Gänswein, would describe the papacy as being, after Benedict's abdication, an "expanded," "quasi-shared" ministry with "an active member and a contemplative member." Pentin

36   Politi, *Pope Francis Among the Wolves*, 29, 35.

37   Diat, *L'Homme*, 63.

38   Timothy Gordon, "The Next Pope with Edward Pentin," YouTube video, 26:10, August 13, 2020, https://www.youtube.com/watch?v=W4r-x6NHHdE. See 4:35–7:04.

39   Edward Pentin, "Debate Intensifies Over Benedict XVI's Resignation and Role as Pope Emeritus," *Edward Pentin* (blog), March 7, 2020, https://edwardpentin.co.uk/debate-intensifies-over-benedict-xvis-resignation-and-role-as-pope-emeritus/.

would say, "Many believe [that these words] must have been cleared beforehand by Benedict or perhaps even written by him." Amidst a firestorm, Gänswein would later clarify that Benedict had validly resigned the papacy.[40]

Later, in countless ways, things would fall apart.

But for now, on February 11, 2013, Benedict finished his resignation speech, walked down the hall with his head bowed, and ultimately broke down crying in his study.[41]

Lightning struck St. Peter's that day.

Again it struck, and the cosmic immensity of Benedict's act shook the Church.

* * *

But for the St. Gallen mafia and its allies, Benedict's gesture was electric.

Martini, Kasper, Danneels, and Murphy-O'Connor had all eerily hinted, just after his election, of Benedict's capacity to surprise. Now, whether because he wanted to shake up the papal office or because his papacy was like a guillotine and he was like glass, Benedict unleashed a jolt of electricity.

The jolt shot to Germany, where Kasper likened the abdication to "a bolt of lightning out of a clear blue sky." "This resignation was a courageous, noble, and humble act deserving of deep respect," said Kasper—who, about to turn eighty, just happened to make the conclave eligibility deadline by five days.[42]

The jolt surged to Belgium, where Danneels felt admiration for the abdicated pope. He had met with Benedict the September

---

40   Pentin, "Debate Intensifies."

41   Gerard O'Connell, *The Election of Pope Francis: An Inside Account of the Conclave that Changed History* (Maryknoll, NY: Orbis, 2019), 36, NOOK.

42   Walter Kasper, *Pope Francis' Revolution of Tenderness and Love*, trans. William Madges (New York: Paulist Press, 2015), 12, Google Books.

before, in a kind of reconciliation meeting suggested by Martini.[43]
Now, Danneels got to enter a conclave he would have been too
old to attend had Benedict's resignation happened just a few
months later.

The jolt rushed to England, where Murphy-O'Connor
received a phone call from Gerard O'Connell, a vaticanista
friend. "He . . . was taken by surprise, even though he had heard
a rumor a year earlier that this could happen," says O'Connell.[44]

Murphy-O'Connor, notably, would tell the BBC that he
was "surprised but not shocked" by the abdication. "I seem to
remember that back in 2002 [Ratzinger] said to somebody that
one day a pope will have to resign given age and so on," Murphy-
O'Connor declared.[45] Later, O'Connell would quote Ratzinger
as having said in 2002: "Given that we live longer nowadays, I
can foresee that a future pope could resign."[46]

The jolt struck Argentina, where, early in the morning, Bergoglio received his own phone call from O'Connell.
O'Connell's "immediate reaction" had been to phone Bergoglio,
and the Latin American listened in silence.[47]

Bergoglio was seventy-six, and it was often said in those
days that the old cardinal looked "depressed," "tired and
dejected," and "exhausted and weary."[48] But according to historian Henry Sire, Bergoglio had spies in Rome, and his commu-
nication with them rose to "hectic levels" as February 11, 2013
neared. That day, the Latin American was reportedly "exultant"

43   Mettepenningen and Schelkens, *Godfried Danneels*, 481.
44   O'Connell, *The Election of Pope Francis*, 29.
45   BBC, "Cardinal Cormac Murphy-O'Connor on Resignation of Pope
     Benedict," YouTube video, 6:17, February 11, 2013, https://www.youtube
     .com/watch?v=A3puol6eacw. See 0:49.
46   O'Connell, *The Election of Pope Francis*, 34.
47   O'Connell, *The Election of Pope Francis*, 28–29.
48   Politi, *Pope Francis Among the Wolves*, 40–41.

as the phone kept ringing "with international calls" of "personal congratulations" from his allies.[49]

"You don't know what this means," Bergoglio told one of them.[50] Then, in the papers, Bergoglio hailed Benedict's abdication as the "revolutionary act" of someone who had been deemed a "conservative pope."[51]

And the jolt made its way throughout Italy—where, in a major paper, Martini's biographer Marco Garzonio said the late cardinal would have appreciated Benedict's abdication. Garzonio pointed out that at their April 2011 meeting, Martini had urged Benedict to take "prophetic actions."[52]

Martini had counted on Benedict, whom he helped to elect, to provide new "surprises," Garzonio said. In his 2012 biography of Martini, Garzonio spoke of the cardinal's realism during the 2005 conclave—of how Martini ultimately confided to friends that, given the conservative orientation of the college of cardinals, it was necessary to pick an intelligent conservative for pope. Ratzinger's name naturally emerged, and according to Garzonio, Martini believed in the mysterious motions of the Spirit—in the possibility that Ratzinger would change.[53]

All that time, Martini had believed in Ratzinger.

---

49   Sire, *The Dictator Pope*, 45–46.
50   Sire, *The Dictator Pope*, 46.
51   O'Connell, *The Election of Pope Francis*, 53.
52   Garzonio, "Perché Martini Avrebbe Apprezzato L'Addio."
53   Garzonio, *Il Profeta*, 434–435.

II

TIME

9

Dark Horse

"I can still remember walking in, and it looked absolutely magnificent in the Sistine Chapel," he said. "The wonderful frescoes of Michelangelo. *The Last Judgment* on the altar."[1]

He was reminiscing about the 2005 conclave before the 2013 papal election. Over and over again in interviews, he told the story of how "somber" and "dramatic" it was to choose a pope beneath the gaze of Christ in *The Last Judgment*.[2]

Later, letting you in on the secret, he'd explain how every cardinal at a conclave keeps a papal name up his sleeve—just in case.[3] Then the old cardinal—who had said, as a three-year-old, that he wanted to be a doctor or the pope—revealed his own names at the 2005 conclave: Adrian and Gregory.[4]

---

1   Michelle Clifford, "Pope: The Secret World of the Conclave," Sky News, March 11, 2013, https://news.sky.com/story/pope-the-secret-world-of -the-conclave-10452072.

2   The Andrew Marr Show, "Interview: Cardinal Cormac Murphy-O'Connor," February 24, 2013, http://news.bbc.co.uk/2/shared/bsp/hi /pdfs/24021303.pdf.

3   Cormac Murphy-O'Connor, *From the Vision of Pope John XXIII to the Era of Pope Francis* (Redemptorist, 2017). See 32:58.

4   Cormac Murphy-O'Connor, *An English Spring: Memoirs* (London: Bloomsbury, 2015), 153, NOOK.

"And once I woke up in the middle of the night and I thought, what about Cormac the First!" he added.[5]

He was eminently likeable, with glasses and a laugh that made you feel comfortable. He was too old to vote in the 2013 papal election, but the work of a conclave—he liked to say—is done before the cardinals go in.[6]

He was the mafia's Cormac Murphy-O'Connor, and he was the kingmaker.

* * *

On March 1, 2013, Murphy-O'Connor dined with Bergoglio, the conclave's dark horse.[7]

"During the pre-conclave period, a steady stream of papal electors were seen visiting the cardinal in his Roman home, the Venerable English College," *The Tablet* said of Murphy-O'Connor. "One of those was . . . Cardinal Jorge Bergoglio, who, it is understood, had supper with the English cardinal at La Pollarola restaurant."[8]

There, over risotto and wine, Murphy-O'Connor and Bergoglio discussed "the sort of person [they] felt the cardinals should elect."[9]

---

5   Murphy-O'Connor, *An English Spring*, 153.

6   Cormac Murphy-O'Connor, "Popes I've Known," YouTube video, 1:03:38, February 29, 2016, https://www.youtube.com/watch?v=2BOh0sOFZFI&t=1 879s. See 31:32.

7   Gerard O'Connell, *The Election of Pope Francis: An Inside Account of the Conclave that Changed History* (Maryknoll, NY: Orbis, 2019), 122, NOOK. O'Connell places the meeting on March, 1, 2013; Murphy-O'Connor, notably, repeatedly dates it to the "Sunday" before the General Congregations—that is, March 3, 2013. See Murphy-O'Connor, *An English Spring*, 185.

8   "Kingmaker Suppers," *The Tablet*, August 24, 2013.

9   Murphy-O'Connor, *An English Spring*, 185.

"We both agreed that [the Church] needed something different," Murphy-O'Connor later recalled. "How's the Church going to be led by Peter, and who's he going to be?"[10]

According to Murphy-O'Connor's memoir, he did not, at that dinner, "raise the issue" of Bergoglio being a candidate.[11] Yet Murphy-O'Connor did ultimately conclude from that meeting that Bergoglio "could be pope."[12]

A day after that dinner—on March 2—the Italian papers quoted an anonymous cardinal as saying, "Four years of Bergoglio would be enough to change things."[13] Murphy-O'Connor would later repeat that exact slogan, adding, "But pray to God we have him for much longer than that."[14]

"Four years of Bergoglio would be enough to change things." Like an eerie chorus, it followed the dark horse's candidacy everywhere.

"Just before" the pre-conclave meetings known as General Congregations began—that is, shortly before March 4—a "very interesting and influential Italian gentleman" approached his friend, then cardinal Theodore McCarrick.

"He could do it, you know," the Italian said of Bergoglio.

"What could he do?" asked McCarrick.

"He could reform the Church. If we gave him five years, he could put us back on target."

"He's seventy-six."

10 Murphy-O'Connor, "Popes I've Known." See 30:55.

11 Murphy-O'Connor, *An English Spring*, 185.

12 O'Connell, *The Election of Pope Francis*, 123.

13 Andrea Tornielli, "Tentazione Sudamericana," *La Stampa*, March 2, 2013, https://www.lastampa.it/cronaca/2013/03/02/news/tentazione-su damericana-1.36108674. Quoted in Marcantonio Colonna [Henry Sire], *The Dictator Pope: The Inside Story of the Francis Papacy* (Washington, DC: Regnery, 2017), 20, Kindle.

14 Paul Vallely, *Pope Francis: Untying the Knots* (London: Bloomsbury, 2015), 187.

"Yeah, five years, if he had five years the Lord working through Bergoglio in five years could make the Church over again."[15]

The Italian asked McCarrick to "talk up" Bergoglio. McCarrick went on, at the General Congregations, to speak of finding a candidate who would reach out to the poor and be connected to Latin America.[16] According to a media representative for the United States Conference of Catholic Bishops, "Prior to the conclave Cardinal McCarrick . . . was touting the praises of [Bergoglio], whom he had met on his many travels."[17]

Later, Austen Ivereigh—Murphy-O'Connor's former press secretary—would speculate that the Italian was "more likely to be a cleric than not."[18] And "if it were a cleric," Ivereigh thought, "it would likely be [Archbishop Loris] Capovilla"—the former personal secretary to Pope John XXIII.[19]

And later it would emerge that McCarrick—who would be laicized in 2019 for sexual abuse—had a mysterious connection to St. Gallen. According to a victim, McCarrick traveled there

15   Theodore McCarrick, "Who Is Pope Francis?", Villanova University, YouTube video, 1:01:07, October 11, 2013, https://www.youtube.com/watch?v=b3iaBLqt8vg&t=3024s. See 18:20.

16   McCarrick, "Who Is Pope Francis?" See 19:57.

17   Sister Mary Ann Walsh, "Pope Francis Has a Style All His Own," *United States Conference of Catholic Bishops Blog*, March 15, 2013, http://usccbmedia.blogspot.com/2013/03/pope-francis-has-style-all-his-own.html. Blogger Steven O'Reilly pointed out this article in June 2020.

18   Austen Ivereigh (@austeni), "3 points…" Twitter, October 12, 2018, 11:17 p.m., https://twitter.com/austeni/status/1050963651077857281. I am grateful to Steven O'Reilly, who initiated this conversation with Ivereigh, for alerting me to it.

19   Austen Ivereigh (@austeni), "I genuinely don't know…" Twitter, October 12, 2018, 10:46 p.m., https://twitter.com/austeni/status/1050955946577592320.

"on a regular basis—on a yearly basis—probably for twenty years."[20]

Eerily, St. Gallen was emerging as a hidden center of gravity for the conclave. In 2005, mafia members at the conclave had sent back a postcard to another member saying, "We are here in the spirit of Sankt Gallen."[21] Now, that spirit rose up like an invisible hand guiding the selection of the next pope.

* * *

"Nobody thought of him," Murphy-O'Connor said of Bergoglio, with regard to the 2013 papal election. "And then, suddenly, a number of cardinals started rooting for him."[22]

"At the conclave," Murphy-O'Connor continued, "you have the official meetings of all the cardinals. But then outside, you meet secretly with the cardinals, at dinners, behind closed doors, and discuss the candidates. So by the time you actually go into conclave, there's already a number of votes for a particular person."[23]

By March 5, Murphy-O'Connor was promoting Bergoglio at a dinner at the Pontifical North American College's Red Room. The name "didn't catch fire that night," says Ivereigh, noting that one American cardinal "was worried about Bergoglio's age."[24]

---

20 Taylor Marshall, "McCarrick's Victim Speaks Out on McCarrick and St. Gallen," YouTube video, 1:42:49, December 5, 2018, https://www.youtu be.com/watch?v=CvYs6fo-HiE.

21 Maike Hickson, "The Themes of the Synod, the Themes of the Sankt Gallen 'Mafia Club,'" LifeSiteNews, October 24, 2015, https://www.lifesitene ws.com/opinion/the-themes-of-the-synod-the-themes-of-the-sankt-gal len-mafia-club.

22 Murphy-O'Connor, *From the Vision of Pope John*. See 3:12.

23 Murphy-O'Connor, *From the Vision of Pope John*. See 3:22.

24 Austen Ivereigh, *The Great Reformer: Francis and the Making of a Radical Pope* (New York: Henry Holt & Co., 2014), 356, Kindle.

By March 7, Murphy-O'Connor was co-hosting a private gathering of cardinals with the United Kingdom's ambassador to the Holy See. "More than one of [the cardinals] brought up Bergoglio's name," says vaticanista Gerard O'Connell.[25]

By March 10, Bergoglio was telling a Canadian priest, "Pray for me." Asked if he was nervous, Bergoglio replied, "A little bit . . . I don't know what my fellow cardinals are cooking up for me."[26]

By the end of the General Congregations, Murphy-O'Connor was making a final push for Bergoglio. As he put it, "I remember saying . . . Because by this time I had my eye on Bergoglio. And I said, 'Age doesn't matter now, because Pope Benedict has given us an example. And so if the new pope is elderly and he can't carry on because of health, why then he'll be able to resign.' . . . And I said, 'We might look in another continent.'"[27]

According to O'Connell, Murphy-O'Connor spoke specifically of crossing to the Americas—and "many understood he was referring to Bergoglio."[28]

Later that day, the conclave's eve, Murphy-O'Connor made his way to the Vatican apartment of an Italian cardinal. There, a meeting of fifteen or more Bergoglio supporters, including Kasper, took place. As each cardinal affirmed his support and named other likely backers, Martini's former private secretary kept a tally. He counted at least twenty-five votes for Bergoglio.[29]

25   O'Connell, *The Election of Pope Francis*, 171. See also "Dinner Role," *The Tablet*, March 16, 2013, and Catherine Pepinster, *The Keys and the Kingdom: The British and the Papacy from John Paul II to Francis* (London: Bloomsbury, 2017), 69–70, Kindle.

26   Marco Politi, *Pope Francis Among the Wolves: The Inside Story of a Revolution* (New York: Columbia University Press, 2014), 46–47, Kindle.

27   Murphy-O'Connor, "Popes I've Known." See 32:00.

28   O'Connell, *The Election of Pope Francis*, 199.

29   O'Connell, *The Election of Pope Francis*, 204–205. Notably, Kasper admits

On March 12, a storm gripped Rome. Hail rained down. As the cardinals dispersed following the Mass before the conclave, Murphy-O'Connor fell into step beside Bergoglio.

"Watch out, now it's your turn," Murphy-O'Connor said.[30]

"I understand," Bergoglio replied.

He was calm, said Murphy-O'Connor, and "was aware that he was probably going to be a candidate going in."[31]

* * *

"It is generally thought," says historian Henry Sire, "that Pope Benedict's purpose in abdicating was to bring about the succession of Cardinal [Angelo] Scola." But according to Sire, Benedict's plan "failed from the start."[32]

As one cardinal puts it, Benedict ingenuously believed Scola would be elected. But Cardinal Tarcisio Bertone, whom Benedict had long trusted, helped thwart Scola's candidacy.[33]

On the conclave's first ballot, according to a leaked diary, Scola received thirty votes. But Bergoglio received almost as

---

attending the meeting but denies any "networking" during the conclave; he says Bergoglio's name came up very "late" and denounces all "stupid suspicions of manipulation and conspiracy theories." See Maike Hickson, "Cdl. Kasper Denies Any 'Networking' to Elect Francis, Despite Attending Pro-Bergoglio Meeting," LifeSiteNews, April 29, 2019, https://www.lifesitenews.com/blogs/cdl-kasper-denies-any-networking-to-elect-francis.

30   Elisabetta Piqué, *Pope Francis: Life and Revolution: A Biography of Jorge Bergoglio* (Chicago: Loyola Press, 2014), 9, Kindle. See also Murphy-O'Connor, *An English Spring*, 188.

31   Miguel Cullen, "Pope Sent Greetings to the Queen Straight After His Election, Says Cardinal," *The Catholic Herald*, September 12, 2013, https://catholicherald.co.uk/pope-sent-greeting-to-queen-straight-after-his-election-says-cardinal/.

32   Sire, *The Dictator Pope*, 47–48.

33   Nicolas Diat, *L'Homme Qui Ne Voulait Pas Être Pape: Histoire Secrète d'un Règne* (Paris: Albin Michel, 2014), 613.

many: twenty-six, one more than the revolutionaries had cal-culated. The other votes were scattered among numerous contenders.[34]

Then the ballots were burned—sending black smoke, the sign of no pope, into the Roman evening.

By the next morning—March 13—Bergoglio had seized the lead. On the second ballot, he earned forty-five votes, against Scola's thirty-eight. On the third ballot, he earned fifty-six, against Scola's forty-one.[35]

Black smoke billowed out again.

Outside the conclave, some caught wind of the campaign to elect Bergoglio. CNN's Christopher Cuomo revealed on air that he had been "offered up" the name of Bergoglio as "the perfect compromise candidate."

"As we're thinking about if the big names don't deliver early on and they have to look for an alternative, [an] interesting sug-gestion from a retired cardinal: Bergoglio, don't count him out," Cuomo said.[36]

When the cardinals returned to voting that afternoon, Bergoglio was still rising with sixty-seven votes, against Scola's thirty-two. The fifth vote was then annulled because there was one ballot too many.[37] Immediately, another vote was taken.

By the end, Bergoglio had eighty-five votes.[38]

"White smoke! White smoke!" someone shouted to Murphy-O'Connor after he celebrated an evening Mass at his

---

34 O'Connell, *The Election of Pope Francis*, 230.

35 O'Connell, *The Election of Pope Francis*, 243–244.

36 CNN, "Transcripts," March 13, 2013, http://edition.cnn.com/TRANSCR IPTS/1303/13/cnr.05.html.

37 O'Connell, *The Election of Pope Francis*, 249–250. O'Connell quotes John Paul II's *Universi Dominici Gregis* 28 to assert the "full compliance" of the vote with the following conclave rules: "If the number of ballots does not correspond to the number of electors, the ballots must all be burned, and a second vote taken at once."

38 O'Connell, *The Election of Pope Francis*, 251.

titular church, Santa Maria sopra Minerva. It was raining, but the cardinal dove into a car and made his way to St. Peter's to catch a glimpse of the new pope. Soon, when "half of Rome" seemed to be walking towards the square, he abandoned the car and walked, amidst an ocean of umbrellas, to a window overlooking the square's central balcony.[39]

"Some minutes" before the identity of the new pope was announced, Murphy-O'Connor slipped a tip-off to his old spokesman, Ivereigh.

"He told my emissary that, as it had been a short conclave, the new pope could well be Jorge Mario Bergoglio," Ivereigh says.[40]

It was. And upon Bergoglio's election as Pope Francis, McCarrick boasted to CNN, "Many of us had thought of it beforehand, that this might happen. So I was not totally surprised. I was delighted."[41]

But somewhere in the Vatican, Benedict was caught off guard.

"Were you expecting someone else?" author Peter Seewald once asked Benedict.

"Certainly, yes, not anyone in particular, but another, yes," Benedict said.

"Bergoglio was not among them, however."

"No, I did not think he was among the more likely candidates."

"Although they say . . . he was one of the favorites at the last conclave, next to you."

"That is true," said Benedict. "But I thought, that is past."[42]

39   Murphy-O'Connor, An English Spring, 189.
40   Ivereigh, The Great Reformer, prologue.
41   CNN, "Transcripts," March 14, 2013, http://transcripts.cnn.com/TRANS
      CRIPTS/1303/14/ampr.01.html.
42   Benedict XVI and Peter Seewald, Last Testament: In His Own Words,
      trans. Jacob Phillips (London: Bloomsbury, 2016), 29, Kindle.

* * *

Murphy-O'Connor loved to talk about his role in Pope Francis's election, and he became a key source for Ivereigh's 2014 book *The Great Reformer*. This book divulged—almost naively—that "there was" indeed a pro-Bergoglio campaign organized in advance.[43]

The book said that before the conclave, various St. Gallen alumni "got to work, touring the cardinals' dinners to promote their man [Bergoglio], arguing that his age—seventy-six—should no longer be considered an obstacle, given that popes could resign."[44]

"[Murphy-O'Connor] explained to me that such 'lobbying' in favor of one papal contender or another was important in ensuring that he would be given consideration once the voting began," said Ivereigh elsewhere.[45]

Then, in *The Great Reformer*, Ivereigh said of the mafia's alumni, "They had learned their lessons from 2005. They first secured Bergoglio's assent. Asked if he was willing, he said that he believed that at this time of crisis for the Church no cardinal could refuse if asked."[46]

Immediately, Murphy-O'Connor and other mafia alumni "explicitly" denied Ivereigh's account of both a "campaign" and a request for Bergoglio's "prior consent."[47] Kasper said that "Ivereigh's assertion that a certain group of European cardinals had already secured Cardinal Bergoglio's acceptance beforehand in the case he was elected lacks every foundation."[48] And

43   Ivereigh, *The Great Reformer*, 406.
44   Ivereigh, *The Great Reformer*, 354.
45   Austen Ivereigh, "Cormac's Conclave," *The Daily Telegraph*, September 5, 2017.
46   Ivereigh, *The Great Reformer*, 354.
47   O'Connell, *The Election of Pope Francis*, 48.
48   Walter Kasper, *Pope Francis' Revolution of Tenderness and Love*, trans.

in what one journalist calls a "carefully worded" and "distinctly vague" denial, Murphy-O'Connor's spokesperson insisted that "no approach to the then Cardinal Bergoglio in the days before the conclave was made."[49]

Still, Ivereigh claimed that Murphy-O'Connor had said the book was "fine" except for the sole line about Bergoglio's assent. As Ivereigh told an audience:

> Now, what [Murphy-O'Connor, Kasper, Lehmann, and Danneels are] upset about is a line which I put in there which I regret writing, or at least the phrasing of it, I regret. I said that this time, unlike 2005, that they sought [Bergoglio's] consent, now, or his assent.
>
> Now, that implies that they actually went to him and said, "Would you be willing to be a candidate?" And that never happened. And [Murphy-O'Connor,] with whom I used to work, was of course an important source for the book. When he read that he said, "You've gotta really, really . . . well, you know, it's all fine except that line gives that impression."[50]

So Ivereigh issued a partial retraction. He said that "in keeping with conclave rules, [St. Gallen alumni] did not ask Bergoglio if he would be willing to be a candidate."[51]

But why, asked one reviewer, would Ivereigh have written the original line about seeking Bergoglio's assent in the first

---

William Madges (New York: Paulist Press, 2015), 93–95, Google Books.

49 See Damian Thompson, "What is the Truth About Cardinal Murphy-O'Connor and 'Team Bergoglio'?" *The Spectator*, November 25, 2014, https://www.spectator.co.uk/article/what-is-the-truth-about-cardinal-murphy-o-connor-and-team-bergoglio-.

50 Austen Ivereigh, "The Great Reformer: Pope Francis and the Making of a Radical Pope," Berkley Center of Georgetown University, YouTube video, 1:12:53, January 6, 2015, https://www.youtube.com/watch?v=1Z67-EGcFW8. See 20:15.

51 O'Connell, *The Election of Pope Francis*, 48–49.

place, "except as a direct and checked report of what he was told by Murphy-O'Connor"?[52]

Repeatedly, Ivereigh insisted that this was an issue of poor phrasing; he knew that no such approach to Bergoglio ever occurred. "I knew that didn't happen, and I'm really sorry," he told EWTN's Raymond Arroyo.[53]

But somewhere in an old, jaw-dropping blog post from two days after the 2013 election, Ivereigh tells the same original story about an approach to Bergoglio in search of an assent.

"Before or after [Bergoglio's General Congregations speech on March 9], he was approached by some over-80 cardinals who had voted for him on the first and second ballots in 2005, to ask him if he could be willing to be considered in 2013. Having received a favorable answer, the idea of Cardinal Bergoglio spread quickly among a number of different groups," wrote Ivereigh.[54]

This notion of some kind of approach to Bergoglio is not unique to Ivereigh.

On the day of Pope Francis's election, CNN's Cuomo spoke of having received his tip about Bergoglio's candidacy from multiple cardinals, at least one of whom was retired.[55] Two years later, Cuomo confirmed that he "got told" by multiple "retired

---

52   Frank Brennan, "Rise of the Great Reformer: Austen Ivereigh and the Making of Pope Francis," ABC Religion & Ethics, January 6, 2015, https://www.abc.net.au/religion/rise-of-the-great-reformer-austen-ivereigh-and-the-making-of-pop/10098702.

53   EWTN, "The World Over," YouTube video, December 11, 2014, https://www.youtube.com/watch?v=anSyu0dDTtQ. See 16:08.

54   Austen Ivereigh, "Pope Francis: How the Quiet Man Fooled an Army of Pundits," Catholic Voices Comment, March 15, 2013, https://cvcomment.org/2013/03/15/how-the-quiet-man-fooled-an-army-of-pundits/.

55   Christopher Cuomo (@ChrisCuomo), "...didn't I mention Bergoglio...," Twitter, March 13, 2013, 5:56 p.m., https://twitter.com/ChrisCuomo/status/311974046545899520.

bishops" to "watch Bergoglio."[56] Then, in a 2015 CNN special, Cuomo presented additional testimony about a mysterious approach to Bergoglio.

"Now, cardinals who had favored Bergoglio's election in 2005 got another chance. Was he the reformer the church needed? Did Bergoglio even want the job? And was he strong enough to lead the church?" said Cuomo.

"So they sent some people to ask him questions. Someone asked him the question, how is your health?" said Rabbi Abraham Skorka, Bergoglio's friend.[57] Cuomo's prior set-up—"Did Bergoglio even want the job?"—strongly insinuates that this topic of wanting the job of pope was one of the questions broached at that meeting.

But even if the approach to Bergoglio originally described by Ivereigh really did take place, that fact would not invalidate Pope Francis's election, says a canonist respected by historian Roberto de Mattei and vaticanista Sandro Magister.

"The constitution of John Paul II [governing papal elections] does not sanction even a simoniac election with invalidity," says the canonist, Geraldina Boni. "Neither does it do so if the election is the result of pacts, agreements, promises, or other commitments of any kind between cardinals (see the other conjecture of a team of four cardinals thought to have planned Bergoglio's election as advanced recently by Austen Ivereigh in the book *The Great Reformer*)."[58]

---

56 Christopher Cuomo, (@ChrisCuomo), "...I WAS the guy who got told...," Twitter, March 13, 2015, 4:48 p.m., https://twitter.com/ChrisCuomo/status/576500148999696384.

57 CNN, "Transcripts: 'The People's Pope,'" September 26, 2015, http://transcripts.cnn.com/TRANSCRIPTS/1509/26/se.01.html.

58 Sandro Magister, "He is Pope. Elected by All the Rules," *L'Espresso*, January 5, 2015, http://chiesa.espresso.repubblica.it/articolo/1350961bdc4.html?eng=y. See also Roberto de Mattei, "Socci's Thesis Falls Short: Review of 'The Secret of Benedict XVI,'" *Catholic Family News*, January 4, 2019,

Boni was saying that even an election touched by simony—the buying and selling of spiritual things, such as Church offices—was not punished with invalidity under John Paul II's constitution. Similarly, the constitution did not invalidate elections resulting from pacts or the kind of commitments initially described by Ivereigh.

The kingmaker had done it. Two days after the election, the new pope joked to Murphy-O'Connor, "It's your fault. What have you done to me?"[59]

Looking back at the 2005 and 2013 conclaves in his memoir, Murphy-O'Connor would think of how "God writes straight with crooked lines." He would think of how, in 2005, "the overriding feeling was that the Church needed continuity," and "any attempt to change tack" would have met with "fierce resistance." Then he would think of how the "poverty" of the Church under Benedict—all the scandals from sexual abuse and Vatileaks, all the "mounting sense of disarray and dysfunction"—had propelled the cardinals to "turn to a radical reformer."[60]

https://catholicfamilynews.com/blog/2019/01/04/soccis-thesis-falls-short-review-of-the-secret-of-benedict-xvi/.

59 Cullen, "Pope Sent Greetings."

60 Murphy-O'Connor, *An English Spring*, 155.

10

The Ghost of
Cardinal Martini[1]

"Four years of Bergoglio would be enough to change things," they had said. And with that, some mysterious hand wound up the timer for Pope Francis's pontificate and the inexorable tick began following him everywhere.

It followed him as he got dressed before making his first appearance as pope at St. Peter's loggia. "No, thank you," he said as the dressing assistant offered him the crimson mozzetta of the popes. Then he refused to exchange his black shoes for red ones, color of the martyrs' blood.[2]

When he came out all dressed in white, wearing his own cross and silver ring instead of the gold pectoral cross of the

---

1   For Edward Pentin's evocative use of this phrase, see "Have Synods Become Vehicles for Legitimizing Heterodoxy?" *The National Catholic Register*, August 25, 2018, https://www.ncregister.com/blog/have-synods-become-vehicles-for-legitimizing-heterodoxy.

2   Elisabetta Piqué, *Pope Francis: Life and Revolution: A Biography of Jorge Bergoglio* (Chicago: Loyola Press, 2014), 30, Kindle.

pope, the other cardinals were "astonished," says his biographer and friend, Elisabetta Piqué.[3]

The ticking kept pursuing the pope with round glasses as he said, "Brothers and sisters, *buona sera*." He was casual, a little shy. "You know that the duty of the conclave was to provide Rome with a bishop," he said.

It was the first of many times that he would call himself not pope but "bishop of Rome."

"The diocesan community of Rome now has its bishop: thank you!" he soon added, resuming the theme. "And now, we take up this journey: bishop and people. The journey of the Church of Rome," he said too.[4]

The language about the "bishop of Rome" was so pronounced, so insistent, that it felt almost scripted. It felt as though then cardinal Theodore McCarrick was right when he said of Pope Francis and his opening gestures, "This is a brilliant man, this is a man who plots the strategy of the Church as it goes along."[5]

Martini biographer Marco Garzonio, meanwhile, saw the echo of someone familiar in the new pope. Like the rest of the world, Garzonio knew little to nothing about the pope from Argentina.

But he says he saw, in those opening gestures of Pope Francis, something of the spirit of Martini.[6]

---

3   Piqué, *Pope Francis*, 30.

4   "First Greeting of the Holy Father Pope Francis," Vatican website, March 13, 2013, http://www.vatican.va/content/francesco/en/speeches/2013 /march/documents/papa-francesco_20130313_benedizione-urbi-et-orbi.html.

5   Theodore McCarrick, "Who Is Pope Francis?", Villanova University, YouTube video, 1:01:07, October 11, 2013, https://www.youtube.com/wa tch?v=b3iaBLqt8vg&t=3024s. See 34:40.

6   TV2000it, "L'eredità del Cardinal Martini," YouTube video, 27:14, February 20, 2017, https://www.youtube.com/watch?v=Kgg7rL7NR9U.

* * *

Thirty-three years before Pope Francis first stepped out onto the balcony of St. Peter's, Martini, the new archbishop of Milan, planned his entrance into his new city.[7] He had been a shy, bookish biblical scholar; he decided to walk in with only a Gospel in hand. And so the tall archbishop with vivid blue eyes eschewed a limousine to walk the streets among his people. He waved and smiled at the clapping women and schoolchildren, blessing a prison along the way.

Grazie, Martini told the crowd when he reached the cathedral, his arms reaching outward. He looked familiar, down-to-earth. On another man, his clerical cape would have looked like the trappings of a prince; on him, it looked like the ruddy outfit that a boy might casually try on. Later, when he rose to become a cardinal, his sister would distinctly remember how he had complained about the red stockings.[8]

Later, his friend Kasper would likewise joke about how "ridiculous" a pope's red slippers were.[9] In St. Gallen, they wanted to drop, more and more, the trappings of the monarchical, princely Church.

They wanted a new kind of pope—iconoclastic, demystified, normal.

After the Second Vatican Council, it was a kind of primordial dream. As vaticanista Sandro Magister points out, Martini was an heir to the revolutionary spirit of Fr. Giuseppe Dossetti—a

---

7 For footage of Martini's entrance, see *Vedete, Sono Uno di Voi: Carlo Maria Martini*, directed by Ermanno Olmi (Italy: Rai Cinema, 2017), DVD.

8 Maris Martini Facchini, *L'Infanzia di un Cardinale: Mio Fratello Carlo Maria. Ricordi e Immagini di Vita Familiare* (Milan: Ancora, 2018), loc. 470 of 1202, Kindle.

9 Paul Elie, "The Pope in the Attic: Benedict in the Time of Francis," *The Atlantic*, May 2014, https://www.theatlantic.com/magazine/archive/2014/05/the-pope-in-the-attic/359816/.

Vatican II innovator who was proud "to have reversed the fortunes of the Council itself at the decisive moment." In 1978, to prepare for the next conclave, a mysterious memo inspired by Dossetti was sent to the cardinal-voters.[10]

It was a script for a new pope's first hundred days.

The new pope—the memo said—needed to act less like a king and more like a normal person who shows himself "for what he really is." He needed to give up "monarchical symbols of power and authority." He needed to stop hiding his true person behind the "morass" of papal accoutrements—the papal residence, the clothing, the titles.

The new pope needed to affirm that he was first and foremost the "Bishop of Rome."

He needed to pursue "collegial governance"—gathering an advisory body of "no more than twelve members."

He needed to recognize "the true and proper legislative capacity of the synod of bishops."

Then the new pope needed to "free himself from the fear" of the Sexual Revolution, from the need to condemn it "mercilessly."

For somehow, the forsaken red shoes and mozzetta seemed to lead, finally, to this point: a white flag before the dictatorship of relativism.

* * *

The ticking followed Francis as, soon after the conclave, he made his way to pay his own hotel bill. It followed as he picked up the phone to cancel his newspaper subscription in Argentina. It followed as he eschewed the papal palace to live in the Vatican's

---

10   Sandro Magister, "Goodbye, King Pope. The Progressivists' Plan at the Conclave," *L'Espresso*, March 1, 2005, http://chiesa.espresso.repubblica .it/articolo/21473%26eng%3dy.html. All subsequent quotations of this memo are from this source.

guesthouse—acting normal, demystifying the papacy.

The ticking continued as, four days after his election, he called Cardinal Óscar Rodríguez Maradiaga.

"Come over for lunch, here at Santa Marta," said Francis to Maradiaga.

"Why in the world would the pope invite me to lunch just four days after his election?" Maradiaga wondered.

When the time for lunch came, Francis was direct. "I thought I would create a council of cardinals," he said. "Do you feel like coordinating the council?" he asked, already holding every name in his head.[11]

Francis was clearly acting according to some program. He was a meticulous planner. Once asked what he'd save from a burning building, he said, "My breviary and my agenda."[12]

"He's an organized man, careful, methodical—'he doesn't take a step without thinking about it first,' as the people who know him say," says Piqué.[13]

The ticking rose as, traveling back from World Youth Day at Rio de Janeiro, Pope Francis gave his first press conference. Asked about Communion for the divorced and civilly remarried, the pope said that the "problem" needed to be "studied."[14]

Asked about his promotion of a cleric accused of having a history of homosexual affairs, Pope Francis said he had scrutinized the man's record and found nothing. Francis could have ended his answer there, as author Phil Lawler points out. But,

11 Óscar Rodríguez Maradiaga, *Only the Gospel is Revolutionary: The Church in the Reform of Pope Francis*, trans. Demetrio Yocum (Collegeville, MN: Liturgical Press, 2018), loc. 619 of 1297, Kindle.

12 Francesca Ambrogetti and Sergio Rubin, *Pope Francis: His Life in His Own Words* (New York: G.P. Putnam's Sons, 2010), 160, Kindle.

13 Piqué, *Pope Francis*, 1.

14 "Full Transcript of Pope's In-Flight Press Remarks Released," *Catholic News Agency*, August 5, 2013, https://www.catholicnewsagency.com/news/full-transcript-of-popes-in-flight-press-remarks-released.

Lawler says, Francis pressed on, "apparently wanting to say something about homosexuality."[15]

"If a person is gay and seeks the Lord and has good will, well who am I to judge them?" the pope said.

"Who am I to judge?" It became an instant, self-interpreting mantra for relativism, plastered on sleek magazine covers next to Francis's smiling face. But listening to the phrase, Italian writer Antonio Socci heard the voice of someone else.

In *Night Conversations*, Martini had said that it would "never occur" to him to "judge" same-sex couples. Now, Socci had the sense that Francis was following *Night Conversations* as if it were his "canvas."[16]

* * *

Four years earlier, in 2009, Martini sat with atheist Eugenio Scalfari for a prophetic interview.[17]

Old and ill from Parkinson's, Martini was shaky at various points, but the spirit inside of him was young and still on fire.

First, Martini promised that he was not there to proselytize his atheist interviewer.[18]

Then Martini recalled a consistory where there had been a debate on the future pope's identity before the 2005 conclave. When it was his turn to speak, Martini said the cardinals had to elect "the bishop of Rome." For Martini wanted to highlight the pope's "pastoral"—not "theological"—capacity.[19]

---

15   Philip Lawler, *Lost Shepherd: How Pope Francis is Misleading His Flock* (Washington, DC: Regnery Gateway, 2018), loc. 368 of 3254, Kindle.

16   Antonio Socci, *Non è Francesco. La Chiesa Nella Grande Tempesta* (Milan: Mondadori, 2015), 240–246.

17   Eugenio Scalfari, *Il Dio Unico e la Società Moderna: Incontri con Papa Francesco e il Cardinale Carlo Maria Martini* (Torino: Einaudi, 2019), 16–21.

18   Scalfari, *Il Dio Unico*, 15.

19   Scalfari, *Il Dio Unico*, 20.

It sounded like something Rahner had wanted: to reduce the pope's doctrinal ministry. It sounded like a Rahnerian "secularization" of the papacy, whereby the pope progressively ignores his task of providing doctrinal clarity.[20]

Scalfari, for his part, thought Martini's talk sounded subversive.

He asked the cardinal about a "Vatican III."

Martini said he did not dream of a Vatican III. Certainly, Vatican II had lost some momentum; but to resume course, a Vatican III was not necessary.[21]

Then Martini revealed his real dream: a council on the divorced, followed by other councils on specific themes. Scalfari asked Martini to list the problems in order of importance.[22]

First, Martini said, came the Church's approach toward the divorced.

Second came the appointment of bishops.

Third came priestly celibacy and the role of the laity.

Fourth came the relationship between politics and the hierarchy.[23]

Then, having delivered his blueprint, Martini smiled, his intense blue eyes illuminating his face.

* * *

In October 2013, Francis sat for his own interview with Scalfari.[24]

---

20 See Socci, *Non è Francesco*, 240–246 and Stefano Fontana, *La Nuova Chiesa di Karl Rahner: Il Teologo che ha Insegnato ad Arrendersi al Mondo* (Verona: Fede & Cultura, 2017).

21 Scalfari, *Il Dio Unico*, 20.

22 Scalfari, *Il Dio Unico*, 20, 16.

23 Scalfari, *Il Dio Unico*, 16.

24 Eugenio Scalfari, "The Pope: How the Church Will Change," *La Repubblica*, October 1, 2013, https://www.repubblica.it/cultura/2013/10/01/ne ws/pope_s_conversation_with_scalfari_english-67643118/.

While the interview, as published, was reconstructed from Scalfari's memory, a Vatican spokesman confirmed that the overall meaning was accurate.[25]

After shaking Scalfari's hand, Francis smilingly told the atheist, "Some of my colleagues who know you told me that you will try to convert me."

"It's a joke," Scalfari replied, answering that his own friends said it was the pope who wanted to convert *him*. Then Francis smiled again and said, "Proselytism is solemn nonsense."[26]

The ghost of Cardinal Martini had come. Asked about St. Ignatius of Loyola, founder of the Jesuits, Francis pivoted to the topic of Martini. "I'd like to remind you that Carlo Maria Martini also came from that order, someone who is very dear to me and also to you," Francis said.[27] A few months earlier, Francis had said that Martini was a "father for the whole Church" and it was an "act of justice" to honor one's father.[28]

Now, asked about St. Francis of Assisi, the pope again invoked Martini.

"I'm not Francis of Assisi and I do not have his strength and his holiness. But I am the Bishop of Rome and pope of the Catholic world," Pope Francis said. "The first thing I decided was to appoint a group of eight cardinals to be my advisers. Not

25   Andrea Gagliarducci, "Pope's Words in Interview May Not Have Been His Own, Scalfari Says," *Catholic News Agency*, November 21, 2013, https://www.catholicnewsagency.com/news/28502/popes-words-in-interview-may-not-have-been-his-own-scalfari-says. According to Gagliarducci: "After the interview was published, Vatican press director Fr. Federico Lombardi maintained that the text was overall faithful to the pope's thought, even though it could not be considered part of his Magisterium."

26   Scalfari, "The Pope: How the Church Will Change."

27   Scalfari, "The Pope: How the Church Will Change."

28   Thomas C. Fox, "Francis Hails Late Cardinal Carlo Martini," *The National Catholic Reporter*, September 2, 2013, https://www.ncronline.org/blogs/francis-chronicles/francis-hails-late-cardinal-carlo-martini.

courtiers but wise people who share my own feelings. This is the beginning of a Church with an organization that is not just top-down but also horizontal."[29]

Then he added, "When Cardinal Martini talked about focusing on the councils and synods he knew how long and difficult it would be to go in that direction. Gently, but firmly and tenaciously."[30]

After that interview, Garzonio said that the new pope was trying to get Martini's synodal dream "onto its feet" so that it could be "turned into reality." Magister dubbed Francis the "Martini pope."[31]

In October 2013, Francis announced a 2014 extraordinary synod on the family. And with that, the father's dream rose in Francis while the timer ticked.

29   Scalfari, "The Pope: How the Church Will Change."
30   Scalfari, "The Pope: How the Church Will Change."
31   Sandro Magister, "Martini Pope. The Dream Come True," L'Espresso, October 15, 2013, http://chiesa.espresso.repubblica.it/articolo/1350623bdc4 .html?eng=y.

11

God of Surprises

Kasper was sitting in front of the television when he heard Francis praise his work during the pope's first Angelus address.[1]

"In these days, I have been able to read a book by a cardinal—Cardinal Kasper, a talented theologian, a good theologian—on mercy," Francis said. "And it did me such good, that book."[2]

"Holy Father, you should not recommend that book! There are many heresies in it!" an old cardinal later said. Smiling, Francis said to Kasper, "It goes in one ear and out the other."[3]

---

1   Walter Kasper, *Essential Spiritual Writings*, ed. Robert A. Krieg and Patricia C. Bellm (Maryknoll, NY: Orbis, 2016), loc. 212 of 2844, Kindle.

2   "Full Text: Pope Francis' First Angelus Address," *Catholic World Report*, March 17, 2013, https://www.catholicworldreport.com/2013/03/17/full-text-pope-francis-first-angelus-address/.

3   David Gibson, "Cardinal Kasper is Enjoying the Spotlight, and Taking Heat, as the 'Pope's Theologian,'" *The Washington Post*, May 15, 2014, https://www.washingtonpost.com/national/religion/cardinal-kasper-is-enjoying-the-spotlight-and-taking-heat-as-the-popes-theologian/2014/05/15/133a04c2-dc66-11e3-a837-8835df6c12c4_story.html.

And with that, just four days into Francis's pontificate, Kasper was back.

Kasper began meeting with Francis every few weeks.[4] His book on mercy flew off the shelves. Kasper's face smiled from the papers, his eyes framed by rimless glasses.

The papers noticed how serendipity itself seemed to smile upon Kasper. Slated to turn too old to vote for a new pope on March 5, 2013, Kasper had made the conclave cutoff by just five days. Assigned a room across from Bergoglio's during the conclave, Kasper had stumbled onto the future pope's radar by sharing a Spanish copy of his book *Mercy*.[5]

But as Kasper and others revealed after Francis's election, that fortuitous encounter was, in fact, preceded by years of contact. By the time of the conclave, Kasper had already met Bergoglio in Argentina, visited him several additional times in Buenos Aires,[6] and watched the Latin American as a member of the St. Gallen circle.

Sometimes serendipity is aided by a little planning.

* * *

In February 2014, handpicked by Francis, Kasper gave an address that effectively set the agenda for the October 2014 synod on the family. Before a consistory of cardinals, Kasper dusted off the project of his heart: the Kasper proposal to open up Communion to the divorced and civilly remarried.

---

4   Paul Elie, "How Pope Francis Became the People's Pontiff," *Vanity Fair*, September 14, 2015, https://www.vanityfair.com/news/2015/09/pope-fr ancis-usa-tour.

5   David Gibson, "Cardinal Kasper is the Pope's Theologian," *National Catholic Reporter*, June 3, 2014, https://www.ncronline.org/news/ vatican/cardinal-kasper-popes-theologian.

6   Thomas G. Case, "As Gentle Rain from Heaven," *The Tablet*, March 15, 2014.

"It's important to note," says German journalist Paul Badde, "that nothing is new about what Kasper is declaring [in the Kasper proposal]. He was talking about this in the early 1990s, but then it was a dispute between him and Cardinal Ratzinger. He was angry at Ratzinger, that he had won the day. Now, Ratzinger can't say anything anymore, so [Kasper's] time has come."[7]

It had come. Back before the 2005 conclave—in a thinly veiled attack against Ratzinger—Kasper had exhorted the other cardinals not to elect a pope who was too afraid of the world. Ratzinger and Kasper, says writer Paul Elie, were locked in a larger dispute over what a pope actually was.

"Kasper argued that the pope is chiefly the bishop of Rome: eminent, yes, but one bishop among many," says Elie. "Ratzinger argued that the pope is a super-bishop of sorts, whom the other bishops must follow as a sign of Church unity."[8]

At first, says Elie, Ratzinger won the dispute, being elected pope after denouncing the dictatorship of relativism. But by 2013, Pope Francis was taking Kasper's side, calling himself bishop of Rome.

"By making clear that the Church—and the papacy—must change with the times, [Francis] is putting a stop to John Paul and Benedict's long effort to make Church doctrine an adamantine bulwark against relativism," Elie says.[9]

So in February 2014, before the cardinals, Kasper grappled with Benedict's shadow. In 1994, Ratzinger had said that the

---

7   Edward Pentin, "Still Controversial: Cardinal Danneels and the Conclave of 2005," *The National Catholic Register*, November 5, 2015, www.ncregis ter.com/news/still-controversial-cardinal-danneels-and-the-conclave-of -2005-9bx1q46a.

8   Paul Elie, "The Pope in the Attic: Benedict in the Time of Francis," *The Atlantic*, May 2014, www.theatlantic.com/magazine/archive/2014/05 /the-pope-in-the-attic/359816/.

9   Elie, "The Pope in the Attic."

divorced and civilly remarried could receive spiritual but not sacramental Communion. But if "someone who receives spiritual communion is one with Jesus Christ," why "can he not also receive sacramental Communion?" Kasper asked.[10]

In fact, Kasper said, a 1972 article by Ratzinger indicated a "means of escape from the dilemma" on Communion. For Ratzinger had once endorsed, in his own words, "that type of indulgence which emerges in [St.] Basil, where, after a protected period of penance, the 'digamus' (meaning someone living in a second marriage) is granted communion without the annulment of the second marriage."[11] And with that, Kasper left Benedict linked to a position that the latter had repeatedly corrected through the years.[12]

Later, Kasper could be heard boasting that he had "coordinated" his proposals with Francis.[13] Pope Francis, meanwhile, effused about how Kasper's work embodied "theology on one's knees."

One day, the pope placed a call to a woman civilly married to a divorced man. The woman publicly claimed—with no

---

10   Sandro Magister, "Kasper Changes the Paradigm, Bergoglio Applauds," *L'Espresso*, March 1, 2014, https://chiesa.espresso.repubblica.it/articolo /1350729bdc4.html.

11   Sandro Magister, "In the Synod on the Family Even the Pope Emeritus Is Speaking Out," *L'Espresso*, December 3, 2014, http://chiesa.espresso.repu bblica.it/articolo/1350933bdc4.html?eng=y.

12   See Carl Bunderson, "Scholars: No, Benedict XVI Doesn't Support Kasper in Synod Debates," *Catholic News Agency*, November 25, 2014, https:// www.catholicnewsagency.com/news/31002/scholars-no-benedict -xvi-doesnt-support-kasper-in-synod-debates. According to Bunderson, even before Ratzinger shut down the Kasper proposal in 1994, he "quickly retracted the 'suggestions' of his 1972 essay as no longer tenable, because they were made 'as a theologian in 1972.'"

13   Sandro Magister, "The True Story of This Synod. Director, Performers, Assistants," *L'Espresso*, October 17, 2014, http://chiesa.espresso.repubblica .it/articolo/1350897bdc4.html.

denials from Francis—that "Father Bergoglio" said she could receive Communion "without problems."[14]

"Benedict knows, better than anybody, that his renunciation of the papacy is what made Francis's freestyle, judgment-averse pontificate possible," says Elie in an article on Benedict entitled "The Pope in the Attic." "The thought is enough to keep him awake at night. For it is his firm belief that the willingness to suspend judgment is the core of the dictatorship of relativism."[15]

* * *

On October 13, 2014, the clock ticked more implacably than ever. It was the ninety-seventh anniversary of the miracle of Fatima, the day that two Italian political parties endorsed same-sex unions,[16] and the release date of the family synod's midterm report.

That morning, Pope Francis made his meditation on the "God of surprises."

Martini had spoken of being "open" to the "surprises of the Holy Spirit."[17] Now, Francis said Jesus had scolded the doctors of the law "for not being open to the God of surprises." How they "had forgotten that they were a people on a journey!" he said. "When one is on a journey one always finds new things, things

---

14   Joshua McElwee, "Pope's Call to Woman Raises Questions on Divorced and Remarried," *The National Catholic Reporter*, April 23, 2014, www .ncronline.org/blogs/ncr-today/popes-call-woman-raises-questions-divorced-and-remarried.

15   Elie, "The Pope in the Attic."

16   Sandro Magister, "Omosessualità. Contro la 'Relatio' Anche San Paolo Dice la Sua. E Anche L'ISTAT," *L'Espresso*, October 15, 2014, http://magis ter.blogautore.espresso.repubblica.it/2014/10/15/omosessualita-sulla-rel atio-anche-san-paolo-dice-la-sua-e-anche-listat/.

17   Carlo Maria Martini and Georg Sporschill, *Night Conversations with Cardinal Martini*, trans. Lorna Henry (New York: Paulist Press, 2012), 48, NOOK.

one does not know." Then Francis remembered how Jesus had called the closed-hearted an "evil generation."[18]

Later that day, like a tremendous "earthquake," the synod's midterm report convulsed the Church.[19] With the report—which advanced the Kasper proposal and more—the Sexual Revolution "officially invaded the Church."[20]

One section of the report spoke prominently of the "precious support" found in same-sex relationships.[21] As this report was read aloud, Archbishop Bruno Forte exchanged a very noticeable thumbs-up sign with another synodal father.[22] Handpicked by Francis to help lead the synod, Forte was a leading disciple of Martini—who had publicly endorsed same-sex civil unions shortly before his death.[23]

When another synodal official was asked about the passages on homosexuality, he gestured toward Forte. "He who wrote the text must know what it is talking about," the official said.[24]

---

18   Pope Francis, "The God of Surprises," Vatican website, October 13, 2014, http://www.vatican.va/content/francesco/en/cotidie/2014/documents /papa-francesco-cotidie_20141013_the-god-of-surprises.html.

19   John Thavis, "A Pastoral Earthquake at the Synod," *John Thavis* (blog), October 12, 2014, https://www.johnthavis.com/post/a-pastoral-earthqu ake-at-the-synod.

20   Roberto de Mattei, "The Need To Resist Heretical Tendencies," *Rorate Caeli* (blog), October 15, 2014, https://rorate-caeli.blogspot.com/2014 /10/de-mattei-on-synod-relatio-need-to.html.

21   "Relatio Post Disceptationem for 2014 Synod of Bishops on the Family," *National Catholic Reporter*, October 15, 2014, https://www.ncronline.org /news/vatican/relatio-post-disceptationem-2014-synod-bishops-family, 52.

22   Philip Lawler, *Lost Shepherd: How Pope Francis is Misleading His Flock* (Washington, DC: Regenery, 2018), loc. 1577 of 3254, Kindle.

23   Carlo Maria Martini and Ignazio Marino, "Il Cardinale Martini: Io e i Gay," *L'Espresso*, March 23, 2012, https://espresso.repubblica.it/palazzo /2012/03/23/news/il-cardinale-martini-io-e-i-gay-1.41690.

24   Edward Pentin, *The Rigging of a Vatican Synod?* (San Francisco: Ignatius Press, 2015), loc. 2450 of 3138, Kindle.

But Forte's revolution wasn't just his own. Ultimately, it emerged that Pope Francis himself had read and approved the midterm report before it was released.[25] And Francis—according to Forte—at some point apprised him of his plan to push forward the Kasper proposal.

"If we speak explicitly about Communion for the divorced and remarried," said Forte, quoting Francis, "you do not know what a terrible mess we will make. So we won't speak plainly; do it in a way that the premises are there, then I will draw out the conclusions."

"Typical of a Jesuit," Forte later joked.[26]

After the midterm report's release, some conservative bishops reportedly went to Benedict, requesting his intervention.[27]

Other synodal participants and observers felt their eyes were being opened.

"It was then that I realized," said one senior Vatican source to vaticanista Edward Pentin. "It wasn't like a jaw-dropping moment because one suspected. But this was it. This made me realize it's all about [Francis]. This is his proposal and he's not neutral."[28]

* * *

During his time in Buenos Aires, according to vaticanista

25 Hilary White and Patrick Craine, "Pope Francis Approved Family Synod's Controversial Mid-term Report Before Publication: Synod Chief," LifeSiteNews, January 29, 2015, https://www.lifesitenews.com/news/pope-francis-approved-family-synods-controversial-mid-term-report-before-pu.

26 Steve Skojec, "Forte: Pope Did Not Want to Speak 'Plainly' Of Communion for Remarried," OnePeterFive, May 7, 2016, https://onepeterfive.com/pope-speaking-plainly-communion-divorced-messy/.

27 Ross Douthat, To Change the Church: Pope Francis and the Future of Catholicism (New York: Simon & Schuster, 2018), 108, Kindle.

28 Pentin, Rigging of a Vatican Synod?, loc. 238 of 3138.

Sandro Magister, then cardinal Bergoglio had already enacted what Kasper had spent decades theorizing. "With no fuss and without making this decision public," Bergoglio "encouraged his priests not to deny Communion to anyone, whether they be married, or cohabiting, or divorced and remarried."[29]

As one slum priest told Paul Vallely, "When you're working in a shanty-town ninety percent of your congregation are cohabiting or divorced. You have to learn to deal with that. Communion for the divorced and remarried is not an issue there. Everyone takes Communion."[30]

Known as a conservative, Bergoglio did not codify, in a public text, this practice on Communion. He just did it. For Bergoglio was already a man of praxis, enacting Marx's famous words: "It is in practice that man must prove the truth, that is, the reality and power, the this-sidedness [this-worldliness] of his thinking."[31] Bergoglio was already, as de Mattei might say, the "true revolutionary." The future pope was changing the Church in practice, actualizing the theories of his "grandfather," Karl Rahner, and his "father," Martini.[32]

---

29   Sandro Magister, "The Man Who Had To Be Elected Pope," OnePeter-Five, April 2, 2017, https://onepeterfive.com/man-elected-pope/.

30   Paul Vallely, "Pope Francis and the Synod: Changing the Way the Catholic Church Makes Its Decisions," The Tablet, 2015, https://www.thetablet.co.uk/UserFiles/Files/Tablet2015lectureONLINEVERSION.pdf. See also Paul Vallely, "The Crisis That Changed Pope Francis," Newsweek, October 23, 2014, https://www.newsweek.com/2014/10/31/crisis-changed-pope-francis-279303.html.

31   Quoted in Roberto de Mattei, The Second Vatican Council: An Unwritten Story (Fitzwilliam, NH: Loreto Publications, 2013), loc. 429 of 16572, Kindle.

32   For a discussion of this intellectual genealogy from Rahner to Martini to Pope Francis, see John-Henry Westen, "VIDEO: Professor Roberto de Mattei Explains the Crisis in the Church - Part 1 of 2," LifeSiteNews, June 25, 2019, www.lifesitenews.com/blogs/professor-roberto-de-mattei-explains-the-crisis-in-the-church-part-1-of-2; and "Remnant in Rome:

And according to Magister, "in St. Gallen they knew and were taking note" of Bergoglio's praxis.[33] For the mafia needed the Latin American to execute its fledgling dreams. As Kasper himself once said, "What Francis tries to implement is, to a high degree, in accordance with the thoughts which we [in St. Gallen] had at that time."[34]

At the end of the 2014 synod, the final document's three paragraphs on the Kasper proposal and homosexuality all failed to gain a two-thirds majority, despite being toned down overall. These rejected paragraphs, according to protocols, should have been expunged from the final document.

But Francis, the true revolutionary, had a surprise up his sleeve.

Breaking synodal rules, the pope said that the rejected paragraphs were to remain part of the final document. Unilaterally—says historian Henry Sire—"Pope Francis himself ensured that the 'Kasper Proposal' would remain on the agenda of the Ordinary Synod [of 2015], despite being rejected by the fathers of the Extraordinary Synod."[35]

Shortly after the first synod, Benedict had his progressive 1972 article on Communion for the divorced and remarried removed from his collective works. "But," says author Ross Douthat, "this signal as to where he stood was all that

Michael Matt Interviews Roberto de Mattei," *The Remnant*, February 26, 2019, https://remnantnewspaper.com/web/index.php/articles/item/43 57-remnant-in-rome-michael-matt-interviews-roberto-de-mattei.

33   Magister, "The Man Who Had To Be Elected Pope."

34   Maike Hickson, "Evidence Pope Follows Blueprint to Change Church by Dissident Cardinal who Led St. Gallen 'Mafia,'" LifeSiteNews, March 29, 2019, www.lifesitenews.com/blogs/evidence-pope-follows-blueprint-to -change-church-by-dissident-cardinal-who-led-st.-gallen-mafia.

35   Sire, *The Dictator Pope*, 105.

conservatives would get; if he was really asked to take an active role in the proceedings, he demurred."[36]

For there in the attic, Benedict would remain largely silent.

In May 2015, forty-eight hours after Ireland legally recognized same-sex "marriages," a "shadow synod" brought together various revolutionaries to plot a more radical program for the 2015 synod. As de Mattei notes, "The [shadow synod's] line is the one mapped out by Cardinal Kasper: secularization is an irreversible process which pastoral reality has to adapt to. And for Archbishop Bruno Forte, he who asked for 'the codification of homosexual rights' at the last synod, and who has been confirmed by the pope as special secretary to the synod on the family, 'it is a cultural process of forced secularization in which Europe is fully involved.'"[37]

Meanwhile, Kasper himself said to an Italian paper that the issue of same-sex relationships—"only a marginal topic" at the last synod—had now become "central." He defended the Irish decision as legitimate: "A democratic state has the duty to respect the will of the people; and it seems clear that, if the majority of the people wants such homosexual unions, the state has a duty to recognize such rights.[38]

More and more, the St. Gallen agenda was no longer hiding in the shadows.

---

36   Douthat, *To Change the Church*, 108.

37   Roberto de Mattei, "Ireland—A Post-Mortem Examination," *Rorate Caeli* (blog), May 27, 2015, https://rorate-caeli.blogspot.com/2015/05/ireland-post-mortem-examination-by.html.

38   Maike Hickson, "Cardinal Kasper Defends Ireland's Gay 'Marriage' Decision," LifeSiteNews, May 29, 2015, https://www.lifesitenews.com/news/gay-unions-now-central-to-synod-agenda-after-irish-vote-cardinal-kasper.

12

Man Behind the Curtain

"The Sankt Gallen group is a sort of posh name," Danneels said, holding a microphone in an espresso-toned chair below a giant cross. He looked a little stiff, hunched up, but his voice sounded intimate.

"But in reality we said of ourselves, and of that group: 'the mafia,'" he said.[1]

Danneels's expression of seriousness did not soften as he said it. Some laughs rose up from the audience. His interviewer smiled with a half-nod that said he was not quite sure what to make of that strange statement. Danneels had just confessed.

"There were some bishops, a few cardinals—too many to name," Danneels continued. "Things were discussed very freely, no reports were made, so that everyone could blow off steam."[2]

He was there at the Belgian National Sacred Heart Basilica in Koekelberg for the presentation of his new authorized

---

1   Jeanne Smits, "Cardinal Danneels Admits Being Part of Clerical 'Mafia' that Plotted Francis's Election," LifeSiteNews, September 25, 2015, https://www.lifesitenews.com/news/cardinal-danneels-admits-being -part-of-clerical-mafia-that-plotted-francis.

2   Smits, "Cardinal Danneels Admits."

biography. He was there because, in this second year of Pope Francis's reign—just weeks before the 2015 ordinary synod on the family—he was ready to step out of the shadows.

For many years, a thick cloak of secrecy had shrouded the mafia. According to one of Danneels's biographers, Jürgen Mettepenningen, "Nobody knew anything about [the mafia] but there were suspicions in Rome, where they were 'not amused' to know about this group that we called Sankt Gallen in the biography." Flemish media said the Vatican once sent Cardinal Camillo Ruini to "try and find out the who, what, and where" of the group. He came up empty-handed.[3]

But now, in the press surrounding Danneels's new biography, the secret yearned to be told.

"The election of Bergoglio was prepared in Sankt Gallen, without doubt," claimed another biographer of Danneels, Karim Schelkens. "And the main lines of the program the pope is carrying out are those that Danneels and Co. were starting to discuss more than ten years ago."[4]

"In 2013, in a way this group actually achieved its ends, notably through the choice of Pope Francis," said Mettepenningen. "You can say that through his participation in that group, Cardinal Danneels has been one of those who were the pioneers of the choice of Pope Franciscus. That is why you could see him beaming on the balcony next to the pope in Rome. Since then he has returned regularly to Rome to speak with the pope."[5]

Shortly after the confessions, out fluttered a partial retraction from the biographers. Stressing that the mafia had disbanded in 2006, they insisted that it did not form a formal lobby

---

3   Smits, "Cardinal Danneels Admits."
4   Smits, "Cardinal Danneels Admits."
5   Smits, "Cardinal Danneels Admits."

group in 2013. The election of Bergoglio was not "prepared in St. Gallen"; rather, it "corresponded with the aims of St. Gallen."[6]

* * *

And yet the retraction could not expunge the image of Danneels by Francis's side at St. Peter's loggia on March 13, 2013. It could not erase the impression of Danneels's hands folded in satisfaction, a sliver of a smile etched across his face.

In photos and videos of the event, he is short, standing to the pope's side in the back row, at times half-covered in the shadows of the men around him. He peers out into the square in his red skullcap and thin-rimmed glasses. Even when Francis bows his head and folds his hands to pray, Danneels still tilts his head up and out toward the square. In front of a drawn-up black curtain, Danneels watches, with various quadrants of his face shrouded in shadows.[7]

He looks intense. He looks transfixed by some scintillating reality that no one else can see.

In 1958, as a young priest-scholar, he was present in the square, among the crowd, when the Venetian cardinal Angelo Roncalli had emerged as Pope John XXIII. According to his biography, the young Danneels was impressed with Pope John—so different from the imperial, hieratic Pius XII.[8] Later,

6   Edward Pentin, "Cardinal Danneels' Biographers Retract Comments on St. Gallen Group," *The National Catholic Register*, September 26, 2015, https://www.ncregister.com/blog/cardinal-danneels-biographers-retract -comments-on-st-gallen-group.

7   See, for instance, *The New York Times*, "Conclave 2013: Pope Francis Speech," YouTube video, March 13, 2013, https://www.youtube.com/wat ch?v=pv9jN5eoR7s.

8   Jürgen Mettepenningen and Karim Schelkens, *Godfried Danneels: Biographie* (Antwerpen: Uitgeverij Polis, 2015), 70, https://pure.uvt.nl/ws/po rtalfiles/portal/28312169/Danneels_Polis_FR.pdf.

Danneels longed to see that fresh air again—a less monarchical feel.

In his dreams, he called the new pope Francis.

"Years before the [2013] conclave, he told me that the church needed a Francis as head of the church," a spokesman of the Archdiocese of Mechelen-Brussels once told *The New York Times*.[9]

In 1991, Danneels published "The Joy of Francis," in which he prayed that God would "send us, too, a Francis who . . . sees the evil afflicting the age and is able to cure it." "For on such a person depends the joy and hope of our closing century," he said.[10]

"We need a Francis whose gaze reaches into the heart of each man and woman of our time, a gaze that touches the spot where they are wounded," Danneels added.[11]

"Like St. Francis, we are witnessing the birth of a new world. One century is dying, another is making its presence felt in the pangs of birth. Do we not need another Francis who knows his age and knows how to heal it?" said Danneels too. Then he thought, "Perhaps this physician is in our midst unrecognized, as Jesus was when he stood among the cross on the banks of the Jordan."[12]

* * *

Meanwhile, sometime around 2000, the mafia grew increasingly fixated on the topics of homosexuality, Communion for

9   Gaia Pianigiani, "Godfried Danneels, Liberal Cardinal Tainted by Sex Scandal, Dies at 85," *The New York Times*, March 24, 2019, https://www.nytimes.com/2019/03/24/obituaries/godfried-danneels-dead.html.

10   Godfried Danneels, *Words of Life: Volume 1*, trans. Matthew J. O'Connell (Kansas City, MO: Sheed & Ward, 1991), 11.

11   Danneels, *Words of Life*, 16.

12   Danneels, *Words of Life*, 23.

the divorced and civilly remarried, and the papal succession of
John Paul II. Soon afterwards, at its January 2002 meeting, the
group made Bergoglio a topic of conversation.[13]

Bergoglio had served as the rapporteur at a 2001 synod,
winning the confidence of many mafia members, including
Danneels. This appreciation was mutual, Danneels's biography
says, because the cardinals shared an allegiance to collegiality.[14]

What it meant to esteem "collegiality" became clearer after
the synod. In 2003, for instance, Ratzinger's Congregation
for the Doctrine of the Faith told bishops to give "clear and
emphatic opposition" to legal recognition of same-sex unions
of any kind. "The Vatican document was a classic example of
what the St. Gallen group of cardinals had long criticized as
Roman overreach," says papal biographer Austen Ivereigh.[15]

That year, Danneels sent a secret letter to the Belgian Prime
Minister praising his "approval of a legal statute for a stable
relationship between partners of the same sex."[16] Bergoglio,
meanwhile, received criticism from Rome for failing to oppose
a 2002 Buenos Aires civil unions law that also protected same-
sex couples. According to Ivereigh, Bergoglio "regarded it as a
purely civic, legal arrangement that left marriage unaffected."[17]

The way historian Henry Sire sees it, Bergoglio in this
period was pragmatically aligning himself with the winds of
change. "Pope John Paul II was in decline; there was a wide
assumption that the next pope would be a liberal," says Sire.[18]

13 Mettepenningen and Schelkens, *Godfried Danneels*, 451–454.
14 Mettepenningen and Schelkens, *Godfried Danneels*, 453–454.
15 Ivereigh, *The Great Reformer*, 312–313.
16 Edward Pentin, "Cardinal Danneels Admits to Being Part of 'Mafia' Club
    Opposed to Benedict XVI," *The National Catholic Register*, September
    24, 2015, https://www.ncregister.com/blog/cardinal-danneels-admits-to
    -being-part-of-mafia-club-opposed-to-benedict-xvi.
17 Ivereigh, *The Great Reformer*, 312.
18 Sire, *The Dictator Pope*, 38–39.

But when Ratzinger won the 2005 papal election instead, Danneels had to cry out that the Church was not "ready for a Latin American pope."

It took eight years and a surprise papal abdication for Danneels to get a second chance at announcing the one whose hour had been delayed.

At a press conference shortly before the 2013 conclave, Danneels sketched the profile of his ideal new pope—a man who would pursue decentralization, synodality, a "crown council," perhaps even a Vatican III.

"We need a Francis," Danneels said.[19]

* * *

Like one foretold, Pope Francis came. And when Danneels stood by him on St. Peter's loggia on March 13, 2013, the old cardinal kept staring out into the square, his eyes transfixed by some mysterious point.

What did he see? Did he see, as in a prophetic flash, what Ross Douthat calls the new pontificate's "iconography"—Francis washing prisoners' feet, Francis glowing amidst crowds, Francis embracing a disabled child and a man covered in boils?[20] Did Danneels see how, following his own call for a physician to heal the world, Francis would rise up to bind wounds in the field hospital of the Church?

And did Danneels see, in Francis's rise, his own resurrection from the dead?

A few years earlier—while Danneels was planning for a serene retirement devoted to prayer, art, Bach, Beethoven, and the Beatles[21]—a sexual abuse victim had secretly recorded damning conversations with the cardinal. The victim had been

---

19   Pentin, "Cardinal Danneels' Biographers Retract Comments."

20   Douthat, *To Change the Church*, 65.

21   Mettepenningen and Schelkens, *Godfried Danneels*, 464.

abused by his own uncle, Danneels's episcopal protégé, for over a decade, starting at age five.

"What do you really want?" snapped Danneels on the tape, telling the victim he didn't need to hear his story again. "Do you want this to be made public?" Danneels later asked before answering his own question, saying that "actually it would be better" to hold off on reporting the abuser.[22]

When the victim persisted in requesting Danneels's help in reporting the abuse, the cardinal said only the pope had authority over the bishop—and "the pope isn't that easy to reach." When Danneels suggested that the victim admit his own guilt and seek forgiveness, the man exclaimed, "Who do I have to ask forgiveness from?"[23]

Soon, a priest told the press that he had personally warned Danneels about the abuser long ago. "I remember that the cardinal became angry. He said this wasn't my job and that I should stay out of it," the priest said.[24]

At one point, police raided Danneels's episcopal residence. "For reasons that remain unclear," says Sire, "the seized evidence was declared to have been inadmissible"—even though a commission leader said Danneels's name appeared in some fifty incriminatory dossiers.[25] At another point, police entered the cathedral crypt and searched the graves of two archbishops

22 Tom Heneghan, "Leaked Danneels Tapes with Catholic Sex Abuse Victim Make for Sad Reading," Reuters, August 29, 2010, http://blogs.reuters.com/faithworld/2010/08/29/leaked-danneels-tapes-with-catholic-sex-abuse-victim-make-for-sad-reading/.

23 Heneghan, "Leaked Danneels Tapes."

24 John Allen Jr., "In Belgium, Anti-Pedophile Priest Rips 'Silence and Omissions' of Bishops," The National Catholic Reporter, June 27, 2010, https://www.ncronline.org/blogs/ncr-today/belgium-anti-pedophile-priest-rips-silence-and-omissions-bishops.

25 Sire, The Dictator Pope, 15–16.

after it had been suggested that Danneels had hidden evidence there.[26]

But now, with Pope Francis's election, Danneels spoke openly of his own resurrection.[27]

In one sermon, Danneels borrowed the cry of Jesus on the cross: "My God, why hast Thou forsaken me?" (Mt 27:46). Then Danneels spoke of how Easter arrived nonetheless, because "then came Pope Francis."[28]

Francis soon invited Danneels to be a special papal delegate to the 2014 and 2015 family synods. Danneels's name was listed as second in importance on the Vatican's official list of Francis's personal appointees.

According to journalist Damian Thompson, a senior Vatican source once told him that Francis invited Danneels to the synods "as a thank-you for the votes he helped deliver" for Francis's election.[29]

* * *

Danneels always said that he had not inherited his father's severity, the severity of a schoolmaster. No, he had inherited something of his mother's limitless compassion.[30] So when it

---

26   Heneghan, "Leaked Danneels Tapes."

27   Mettepenningen and Schelkens, *Godfried Danneels*, 487.

28   Mettepenningen and Schelkens, *Godfried Danneels*, 490.

29   Damian Thompson, "Three Things You Need to Know about Pope Francis and the Cardinal Disgraced in a Sex Abuse Scandal," *The Spectator*, October 8, 2015, https://www.spectator.co.uk/article/three-things-you-need-to-know-about-pope-francis-and-the-cardinal-disgraced-in-a-sex-abuse-scandal. See also Damian Thompson (@holysmoke), "For me, alarm bells went off when Danneels attended the Synod in the Family. I asked a cardinal why Francis invited him. 'To thank him for votes'…" Twitter, August 20, 2018, 7:29 a.m., https://twitter.com/holysmoke/status/1031518513658294272.

30   See Godfried Danneels, *Confidences d'un Cardinal* (Bruxelles: Racine, 2009).

came time for Danneels to speak to the 2015 synod, he said something about the mystery of mercy.

Back in 1999, when Martini had announced his "dream" at a synod, Danneels had given a parallel talk on mercy in the context of Communion for the divorced and civilly remarried. "[Danneels] suggested that the Catholic church may need to learn from the Orthodox church, in which the sacraments are understood as 'medicine for the soul,'" says vaticanista John Allen Jr.[31]

Now, in 2015, Danneels dramatically told the synod:

> Deep in every man, in every woman, there is a hidden place where someone lives, someone who always listens and offers a saving word. It is the place where God lives; where His Spirit lives in us. That place is called "the home of mercy."
>
> The Hebrew word for mercy (*rahamin*) does not know the word "heart," but uses the word "womb" (uterus). For in that "womb of mercy" there is tenderness and security, which is even greater than marital intimacy. In God's house, man is secure as in the womb.[32]

"The womb of mercy." Danneels used the expression so naturally, so exquisitely. And yet two different politicians had accused him of once advising the Belgian king to sign a law

---

31   John Allen Jr., "Reopening the Divorce Question," *The National Catholic Reporter*, October 29, 1999, http://natcath.org/NCR_Online/archives/102999/102999g.htm.

32   Quoted in John Zmirak, "Cardinal Danneels: A Wolf in Shepherd's Clothing," *The Stream*, October 18, 2015, https://stream.org/cardinal-danneels-a-wolf-in-shepherds-clothing/.

in favor of abortion.[33] While Danneels denied the charge,[34] he made a distinction between "legal frameworks" and "moral norms" that carved a space, in principle, for legal abortion.[35]

"The womb of mercy." An enthusiastic Danneels promised "tenderness," "security." And yet the sexual abuse victim who secretly recorded Danneels could be heard crying out to him: "Why do you feel so sorry for [my abuser] and not for me? You're always trying to defend him. I thought I was going to get some support, but I have to sit here and defend myself against things I can't do anything about."[36]

"The womb of mercy." It represented a sentimental, short-hand argument for why the Church needed Pope Francis's "revolution of tenderness" in general and the Kasper proposal in particular. But what if you tugged at the curtain behind the pontificate's sweetest tropes about medicine, mercy, and tenderness and found the disgraced Danneels standing there, face half-covered in shadows, looking intense, back after his rising from the dead?

---

33   Jeanne Smits, "Cardinal Danneels Tried to Convince Belgian King to Sign Bill Legalizing Abortion: Former Prime Minister," LifeSiteNews, April 22, 2015, https://www.lifesitenews.com/news/cardinal-danneels-tried-to-convince-belgian-king-to-sign-bill-legalizing-ab.

34   Edward Pentin, "Cardinal Godfried Danneels Dies at 85," *The National Catholic Register*, March 14, 2019, https://www.ncregister.com/blog/cardinal-godfried-danneels-dies-at-85-kk1rxrsn.

35   Smits, "Cardinal Danneels Tried."

36   Heneghan, "Leaked Danneels Tapes."

13

Chekhov's Gun

Chekhov's gun. It is the idea, in drama, that a gun lying motionless on a mantelpiece needs to fire off later.

It is an apt symbol for the destiny of the Kasper proposal.

Since the 1970s, Kasper had crusaded for Communion for adulterers even when the fledgling cause seemed lost. Now, toward the end of the 2015 synod on the family, Kasper was "at the heart of negotiations," a source told *The Washington Post*. Speaking of a "compromise" between Kasper and the conservative Cardinal Gerhard Müller, the paper described a "vaguely worded recommendation" regarding the Kasper proposal in the synod's final document.[1]

Back in his 2014 consistory address, Kasper had said, "It would cause a terrible disappointment if we would only repeat the answers that supposedly have always been given. . . . We should at least open the door a crack."[2] Now, regarding the 2015

---

1   Michelle Boorstein and Anthony Faiola, "Meet the 82-year-old Progressive German Cardinal Who Has an Outsized Influence on Pope Francis," *The Washington Post*, October 29, 2015, https://www.washingtonpost .com/news/acts-of-faith/wp/2015/10/29/meet-the-82-year-old-progress ive-german-cardinal-who-has-the-ear-of-pope-francis/.

2   Walter Kasper, *The Gospel of the Family*, trans. William Madges (New York: Paulist Press, 2014), 44.

final document, Kasper told an Italian paper, "I am satisfied, a door was opened on the possibility [to give Communion to the divorced and remarried]. There's some opening, yes, but consequences haven't yet been talked about. Now it's all in the hands of the pope, who will decide what to do."[3]

And here is where the plot thickens.

In some reports, there is talk of a mysterious lunch where, a few days before the vote on the 2015 final document, it is claimed that Cardinal Christoph Schönborn "received Pope Benedict's encouragement for a sort of compromise between Cardinals Müller and Kasper," as journalist Maike Hickson phrased it. Schönborn denied the reports; other German sources confirmed them.[4] In any case, there would be no further interference on the Kasper proposal from Benedict.

Inevitably, a hand moved closer to the mantelpiece.

And by the dramatist Chekhov's logic, the dangerous object needed to go off.

* * *

It did, in Pope Francis's post-synodal exhortation *Amoris Laetitia*. But the actual sound of the firing was so softened by indirection that not everyone could agree on what had happened.

Had Francis endorsed the Kasper proposal or not in *Amoris Laetitia*? Some heard the piercing clang of revolution. Others just heard some vague, indistinct sound in the distance.

---

3   Boorstein and Faiola, "Meet the 82-year-old Progressive."

4   Maike Hickson, "New Sources Bolster Report that Pope Benedict Played Key Role in Synod Compromise," OnePeterFive, March 12, 2018, https://onepeterfive.com/new-sources-bolster-report-that-pope-benedict-was-involved-in-synod-compromise/. I am grateful to Dr. Hickson for apprising me of this report.

For *Amoris Laetitia*'s argument on Communion rested on circumlocution, on an elaborately rigged chain. At its most basic level, the text said that those in an "objective situation of sin" could receive the Church's "help" (*AL* 305). An earlier section, footnote 329, made it clear that Francis was speaking of sexually active divorced and remarried persons—misrepresenting prior Church documents to question the advisability of living as brother and sister in such cases. Then footnote 351 spoke of two sacraments in the context of "help" for such persons: the Eucharist and confession.[5]

"I would also point out that the Eucharist 'is not a prize for the perfect, but a powerful medicine and nourishment for the weak' (*Evangelii Gaudium* 47)," said Francis in the footnote, in the context of "help" for the divorced and civilly remarried.

"The sacraments are not an instrument of discipline, but rather a help for people in the moments of their journey and in the weaknesses of life," said Martini in 2012, speaking of Communion for the divorced and civilly remarried.[6]

As papal biographer Austen Ivereigh points out, the verbal echoes between Martini and Francis here are striking.[7] Historian Roberto de Mattei, too, has said that Martini's larger speech—his last testament—essentially contains the entirety of *Amoris Laetitia*.[8]

---

5   Pope Francis, *Amoris Laetitia*, Vatican website, April 2016, http://www .vatican.va/content/dam/francesco/pdf/apost_exhortations/documents /papa-francesco_esortazione-ap_20160319_amoris-laetitia_en.pdf.

6   Sandro Magister, "After Martini, the Fight Over His Spiritual Testament," *L'Espresso*, September 6, 2012, http://chiesa.espresso.repubblica.it/artico lo/1350318bdc4.html?eng=y.

7   Austen Ivereigh, *Wounded Shepherd: Pope Francis and His Struggle to Convert the Catholic Church* (New York: Henry Holt, 2019), 188–189, Kindle.

8   Roberto de Mattei, "The Second Vatican Council: A Story Now Being Written," *Catholic Family News*, May 22, 2019, https://catholicfamilyne

So Martini was an interpretive key to *Amoris Laetitia*, another preparer of Chekhov's gun. The text's ventriloquism of Martini's voice would set off revolutions.

In the Philippines, the gun went off early; the bishops' conference said that *Amoris Laetitia* meant that the divorced and civilly remarried could discern a return to the Holy Eucharist.[9] In Philadelphia, the discharge stalled; the archbishop reaffirmed the Church's ancient discipline.[10]

And *Amoris Laetitia* not only tolerated but necessitated this interpretive free-for-all. As the pope himself put it, "Since 'time is greater than space,' I would make it clear that not all discussions of doctrinal, moral or pastoral issues need to be settled by interventions of the magisterium. Unity of teaching and practice is certainly necessary in the Church, but this does not preclude various ways of interpreting some aspects of that teaching or drawing certain consequences from it" (*AL* 3).

"We are in a world of dynamic fluidity here, of starting open-ended processes, of sowing seeds of desired change that will triumph over time," explains scholar Anna Silvas. For if Antonio Gramsci, an originator of cultural Marxism, taught "how to achieve revolution by stealth," Silvas thought that Francis was putting those theories into practice. He was pursuing not a direct change in doctrine but an "incremental change of praxis" across the individual regions of the world, until the

ws.com/blog/2019/05/22/the-second-vatican-council-a-story-now-being-written/.

9   Claire Chretien and John Jalsevac, "Vatican-Approved Magazine: Exhortation Opens Door to Holy Communion for Remarried Divorcees," LifeSiteNews, April 13, 2016, https://www.lifesitenews.com/news/vatican-approved-newspaper-exhortation-allows-holy-communion-for-remarried.

10   Joan Frawley Desmond, "Archbishop Chaput's 'Amoris Laetitia' Guidelines," *The National Catholic Register*, July 15, 2016, https://www.ncregister.com/news/archbishop-chaput-s-amoris-laetitia-guidelines.

praxis would be "sufficiently built up over time to a point of no return."[11]

One day in September 2016, the Argentine bishops of the Buenos Aires region released their guidelines on *Amoris Laetitia*, explicitly saying that sexually active divorced and civilly remarried persons could, with the help of a priest, discern the possibility of receiving the Holy Eucharist. Then it emerged: a leaked private letter from Francis hailing the guidelines, saying there were "no other interpretations" of *Amoris Laetitia*.[12]

"Today the greatest threat to the teaching authority of the pope is the pope himself," said journalist Phil Lawler. After the Buenos Aires letter allowing local clerics to make their own decisions on Communion for adulterers, Lawler said he was questioning whether Francis was "deliberately undermining his own teaching office."

"He has spoken frequently about decentralization of Church authority; does he really mean to go that far?" asked Lawler. "The pope has playfully encouraged young Catholics to 'make a mess;' is he trying to set an example, to deconstruct the teaching office?"[13]

That should have been the play's climax—the deleterious triumph of the Kasper proposal.

11   Anna Silvas, "A Year After 'Amoris Laetitia.' A Timely Word," *L'Espresso*, April 21, 2017, http://magister.blogautore.espresso.repubblica.it/2017/04/21/a-year-after-amoris-laetitia-a-timely-word/.

12   John-Henry Westen and Matthew Cullinan Hoffman, "Pope: 'No Other Interpretation' of 'Amoris Laetitia' Than Allowing Communion for Divorced/Remarried in Some Cases," LifeSiteNews, September 9, 2016, https://www.lifesitenews.com/news/pope-no-other-interpretation-of-amoris-laetitia-than-allowing-communion-for.

13   Phil Lawler, "Is Pope Francis Deliberately Subverting Papal Teaching Authority?" *Catholic Culture*, September 15, 2016, https://www.catholicculture.org/commentary/is-pope-francis-deliberately-subverting-papal-teaching-authority/.

And yet in a section of *Amoris Laetitia* on conscience, philosopher Josef Seifert found what looked like a "theological atomic bomb."

* * *

The explosive was hidden in *Amoris Laetitia*'s section 303, which said conscience could discern that God is "asking" one to commit intrinsic wrongs such as adultery.

As Pope Francis put it, "Yet conscience can do more than recognize that a given situation does not correspond objectively to the overall demands of the Gospel. It can also recognize with sincerity and honesty what for now is the most generous response which can be given to God, and come to see with a certain moral security that it is what God himself is asking amid the concrete complexity of one's limits, while yet not fully the objective ideal" (AL 303).

This text, says Seifert, "appears to affirm clearly that these intrinsically disordered and objectively gravely sinful acts . . . can be permitted, or can even objectively be commanded, by God."[14]

But if *Amoris Laetitia* in fact affirms this, Seifert knew he was peering at something terrible.

He saw that the alarm over its "changes of sacramental discipline" on adulterers referred "only to the peak of an iceberg, to the weak beginning of an avalanche, or to the first few buildings destroyed by a moral theological atomic bomb that threatens to tear down the whole moral edifice of the ten commandments and of Catholic moral teaching."[15]

---

14   Pete Baklinski, "'Amoris Laetitia' is a Ticking 'Atomic Bomb' Set to Obliterate All Catholic Morality: Philosopher," LifeSiteNews, August 23, 2017, https://www.lifesitenews.com/news/amoris-laetitia-is-a-ticking-atomic-bomb-set-to-obliterate-all-catholic-mor.

15   Baklinski, "'Amoris Laetitia' is a Ticking 'Atomic Bomb.'"

A group of four cardinals saw the danger too. In late 2016, they revealed that they had presented Pope Francis with five *dubia*—formal theological questions seeking clarification.

To paraphrase their five yes-or-no questions:

Can the divorced and civilly remarried be admitted to the Holy Eucharist?

Is it still valid to teach that there are absolute moral norms?

Can it still be affirmed that one who habitually violates a commandment (such as that against adultery) is in "an objective situation of grave habitual sin?"

Is it still valid to say that circumstances and intentions can never turn an intrinsically evil act into something "'subjectively' good or defensible?"

Is it still true that conscience can never legitimize "exceptions to absolute moral norms?"[16]

Thick, unbroken silence came from Francis.

This was what it looked like to have a pope who, in line with St. Gallen's aims, called himself primarily the "bishop of Rome," downplayed his doctrinal role, and pursued "decentralization," "synodality," and "collegiality." Francis's silence had an apparent explanation: he was playing the part of the pope who steps back from teaching and clarifying.

Meanwhile, from somewhere in the void—without another voice to counter or correct it—Francis's old 2013 interview with Eugenio Scalfari spoke up.

"Your Holiness, is there is a single vision of the Good? And who decides what it is?" Scalfari asked.

---

16   Edward Pentin, "Full Text and Explanatory Notes of Cardinals' Questions on 'Amoris Laetitia,'" *The National Catholic Register*, November 14, 2016, https://www.ncregister.com/blog/full-text-and-explanatory-notes-of-cardinals-questions-on-amoris-laetitia.

"Each of us has a vision of good and of evil. We have to encourage people to move towards what they think is Good," Francis reportedly said.

"Your Holiness, you wrote that in your letter to me. The conscience is autonomous, you said, and everyone must obey his conscience. I think that's one of the most courageous steps taken by a pope," said Scalfari.

"And I repeat it here. Everyone has his own idea of good and evil and must choose to follow the good and fight evil as he conceives them," Francis said, allegedly.[17]

Another time, in a piece published one Holy Thursday, Scalfari quoted Francis as abolishing hell—for the fourth time. While the Vatican denied that Francis said the following exact words, it would not deny that he communicated their meaning: "Evil souls do not go anywhere in punishment. The souls that repent obtain the forgiveness of God and enter the ranks of the souls that contemplate him, but those that do not repent and therefore cannot be forgiven disappear. There is no hell, there is the disappearance of sinful souls."[18]

* * *

"I hope that sooner or later God redeems everyone. I am a great optimist," said Martini in *Night Conversations*. But regarding sinners such as Hitler, Martini thought it was "easier" to think

17	Eugenio Scalfari, "The Pope: How the Church Will Change," *La Repubblica*, October 1, 2013, https://www.repubblica.it/cultura/2013/10/01/news/pope_s_conversation_with_scalfari_english-67643118/.

18	Sandro Magister, "The Pope and Scalfari: Which Francis Are We Supposed To Believe?" LifeSiteNews, April 5, 2018, https://www.lifesitenews.com/opinion/the-pope-and-scalfari-which-francis-are-we-supposed-to-believe. According to Magister, "It is in any case highly credible that Francis truly said such things to Scalfari, seeing that he reported not once but four times in a row without the pope feeling the need to clarify anything, in each subsequent meeting with his friend."

that "such people are simply extinguished."[19]

Martini was trying to explain how "nobody knows if anyone is" in hell.[20] He was speaking in *Night Conversations* about his philosophy of sin and punishment.

"The Church has talked a lot about sin, too much," Martini said. It was better, he thought, to wage war against "sin in the world."[21] He spoke of his own conscience's "development," of how he was "lucky." His parents and the teachers at his Jesuit school were "strict," but they "didn't instill a guilty conscience" in him.[22]

"The times are long gone," said Martini, "when the Church could talk you into having a guilty conscience."[23]

Then he invoked a decontextualized line from Vatican II: "Conscience is the innermost core and shrine of man, in which he is alone with God" (*Gaudium et Spes* 16).[24]

Long ago, as a new archbishop, Martini had opened up the cathedral to young people for a "School of the Word." In they flocked, in throngs, sometimes up to five thousand in number, spilling into the aisles, tailor sitting on the ground and the altar steps, drawn as if irresistibly to the man in black. They would read a section of Scripture and then sit in silence, each person listening for "his or her own answer."[25]

19 Carlo Maria Martini and Georg Sporschill, *Night Conversations with Cardinal Martini*, trans. Lorna Henry (New York: Paulist Press, 2012), 16, NOOK.

20 Martini and Sporschill, *Night Conversations with Cardinal Martini*, 16.

21 Martini and Sporschill, *Night Conversations with Cardinal Martini*, 26.

22 Martini and Sporschill, *Night Conversations with Cardinal Martini*, 25.

23 Martini and Sporschill, *Night Conversations with Cardinal Martini*, 25.

24 Martini and Sporschill, *Night Conversations with Cardinal Martini*, 26.

25 Martini and Sporschill, *Night Conversations with Cardinal Martini*, 41.

One day after a workshop, Martini cried, "Who among you is prepared to follow completely the will of God?" Some hundred people responded.[26]

Another day, a Jesuit from a magazine asked some young Italians in a train station why they found Martini so attractive.

"He is authentic. We think he is authentic. When he says something, you know that he believes it, and you believe it too," one young woman replied.[27]

And what Martini believed, in *Night Conversations*, was that "we can't teach young people anything. We can only help them to listen to their inner master."[28]

"'Your sons and daughters will prophesy, your young men will see visions, and your old men will dream dreams,'" said Martini, grandiosely quoting the prophet Joel. "The young people will be prophets. . . . By being critical, youth carries us, and especially the Church, forward."[29]

* * *

"In chapter 3, verse 2, the prophet Joel says this to us, as a prophecy: 'The old will dream dreams, and the young will prophesy,' namely, with prophecies they will take concrete things forward," said Pope Francis to a 2017 gathering of young people.[30]

26 Martini and Sporschill, *Night Conversations with Cardinal Martini*, 42.

27 Edward W. Schmidt, "Cardinal Carlo Maria Martini: An Archbishop of the People," *America Magazine*, September 1, 2017, https://www.america magazine.org/arts-culture/2017/09/01/cardinal-carlo-maria-martini-ar chbishop-people.

28 Martini and Sporschill, *Night Conversations with Cardinal Martini*, 45.

29 Martini and Sporschill, *Night Conversations with Cardinal Martini*, 47–48.

30 See "Pope Francis Did It Again," Little Sisters of the Poor website, https://littlesistersofthepoor.org/blog-post/pope-francis-yup-told-young-peop le-talk-grandparents/.

He had called a youth synod for 2018. And he had named, as one of its special secretaries, Fr. Giacomo Costa, SJ—the vice president of the Martini Foundation.

As the synod neared, everything seemed set up for an explosive Act III. In his book on Pope Francis and discernment, Costa had claimed a link between *AL* 303—the location of the atomic bomb on conscience—and the notion of conscience in Vatican II's *Gaudium et Spes* 16 ("Conscience is the innermost core and shrine of man, in which he is alone with God").[31] Now, the youth synod's working document, which Costa helped write, asserted the same linkage between *AL* 303 and *GS* 16.[32]

In early 2018, a papal ally, Cardinal Blase Cupich, had concatenated the very same texts to prophesy a "new paradigm"— one where God's voice, reverberating in one's conscience, "could very well affirm the necessity of living at some distance" from the commandments.[33]

Seizing this new paradigm, the youth synod's working document spoke of opening up the question of "what to suggest" to young same-sex couples. "Some LGBT youths, through various contributions that were received by the General Secretariat of the Synod, wish to 'benefit from greater closeness' and experience greater care by the Church, while some bishops' conferences ask themselves what to suggest 'to young people who decide to create homosexual instead of heterosexual couples,'" said the text.[34] Meanwhile, at various pre-synodal events,

---

31 Giacomo Costa, *Il Discernimento* (Milan: Edizioni San Paolo, 2018), 17.

32 See "Instrumentum Laboris: Synod on Young People, the Faith, and Vocational Discernment," Vatican website, 2018, http://www.synod.va/content/synod2018/en/fede-discernimento-vocazione/instrumentum-laboris-for-the-synod-2018—young-people—the-faith.html, 116–117.

33 For a discussion and critique of Cupich's intervention, see Richard Spinello, "Cardinal Cupich Misreads Vatican II on Conscience," *Crisis Magazine*, February 19, 2018, https://www.crisismagazine.com/2018/cardinal-cupich-misreads-vatican-ii-conscience.

34 "Instrumentum Laboris," 197.

various young handpicked prophets spoke of pursuing the homosexuality debate.[35]

Then the bombshell came.

Shortly before the youth synod started, Archbishop Carlo Maria Viganò accused Francis of covering up sexual abuse by then cardinal Theodore McCarrick. Viganò further accused multiple synodal fathers of complicity in the cover-up.[36] Francis said he would not say one word about the allegations.

At the synod, things grew quiet, tranquil. The explosion on the topic of homosexuality never came—likely because Francis himself defused it, says vaticanista Sandro Magister.[37]

And yet, by Chekhov's logic, the bomb still had to go off.

"It's wrong," said Chekhov, "to make promises you don't mean to keep."[38]

---

35 See, for instance, Angela Markas, "Address to the Pre-Synod Gathering of Young People," *Melbourne Archdiocese Catholic Schools*, 2018, https://www.macs.vic.edu.au/CatholicEducationMelbourne/media/News-Events/RE%20Conference%202018/Address-to-the-Pre-Synodal-Meeting-Angela-Markas.pdf; and Ashleigh Green, "Presentation for International Seminar on Young People," *Australian Catholic Bishops Conference Media Blog*, September 11, 2017, https://mediablog.catholic.org.au/wp-content/uploads/2017/09/Presentation-for-International-Seminar-on-Young-People-Ashleigh-Green.pdf.

36 Diane Montagna, "Pope Francis Covered Up McCarrick Abuse, Former US Nuncio Testifies," LifeSiteNews, August 25, 2018, https://www.lifesitenews.com/news/former-us-nuncio-pope-francis-knew-of-mccarricks-misdeeds-repealed-sanction.

37 Sandro Magister, "Synod. The Pope Has Hit the Brakes, and On Homosexuality the Catechism Still Applies," *L'Espresso*, October 24, 2018, http://magister.blogautore.espresso.repubblica.it/2018/10/24/synod-the-pope-has-hit-the-brakes-and-on-homosexuality-the-catechism-still-applies/.

38 Quoted in Leah Goldberg, *Russian Literature in the Nineteenth Century* (Israel: Magnes Press, 1976), 163.

14

Things Fall Apart

"Incremental change is usually best," Murphy-O'Connor, the kingmaker, liked to say. Then he'd add, in his self-deprecating way, "But perhaps that's just Cormac, always the cautious reformer rather than the reckless revolutionary, talking."[1]

The old cardinal had long been called a "safe pair of hands."[2] But even he still had a few "blots" on his record, he said. The first was a 1984 interview championing the role of subjective conscience in decision-making on contraception. The second was an old penchant for saying "vaguely provocative" things about the priestly ordination of married men.[3]

After the Second Vatican Council, Murphy-O'Connor found himself trying to help steady the boat at the English College in Rome. "Rome was in a ferment," said Murphy-O'Connor. "Everything seemed to be up for grabs. Some of the

---

1   Cormac Murphy-O'Connor, *An English Spring: Memoirs* (London: Bloomsbury, 2015), 160, NOOK.

2   Alex Kirby, "Murphy-O'Connor: Everyone's Favorite," *BBC News*, February 15, 2000, http://news.bbc.co.uk/2/hi/uk_news/642802.stm.

3   Murphy-O'Connor, *An English Spring*, 121, 168.

students thought that the rule of mandatory celibacy for priests, for example, was going to be changed."[4]

And so Murphy-O'Connor had "to broker a peace between the people who want to change everything and the people who want to change nothing." "The trick," he said, "was to let the leash out gently, so that you could allow things to develop while staying in control."[5]

He tried it in 1969. At a synod brimming with radical calls against celibacy, Murphy-O'Connor, feeling a "rush of blood to the head," said in patchy, impromptu Latin that "perhaps the ordination of married men should be considered."[6]

He tried it again before another synod. In a circumlocutory article, Murphy-O'Connor said, finally, that the administration of the sacraments was "of much greater importance" than the law of celibacy.[7]

By 2011, the St. Gallen alumnus had grown less timid.

"If you're asking, 'Can the Church change its laws about celibacy?' the answer is 'Yes,' any time in the next papacy," he told an interviewer.[8] But whether Murphy-O'Connor spoke of change in the "next papacy" out of optimism or plotting, he did not say.

When Benedict abdicated in 2013, Murphy-O'Connor sat for a press conference about electing a new pope. Dressed in black while cameras flashed incessantly, Murphy-O'Connor answered a question about celibacy.

---

4   Murphy-O'Connor, *An English Spring*, 80.

5   Murphy-O'Connor, *An English Spring*, 81.

6   Murphy-O'Connor, *An English Spring*, 75.

7   Cormac Murphy-O'Connor, "Clerical Celibacy," *The Furrow* 20, no. 5 (1969): 1–5, http://www.jstor.org/stable/27678820.

8   John Walsh, "More Tea, Cardinal?" *The Independent*, October 22, 2011, https://www.independent.co.uk/news/uk/this-britain/more-tea-cardin al-554503.html.

"I think that at the moment, celibacy is mandatory," said Murphy-O'Connor, looking down, searching for his qualifiers. "Whether there should be any development with regard to the ordination of married men . . . I think that will be a matter that may well come up sometime or other," he continued, looking up.[9]

The trick was to let the leash out gently.

* * *

As a cardinal under Benedict's reign, Bergoglio, too, knew how to deploy the trick.

"Right now," said Bergoglio in 2010, "I stand by Benedict XVI, who said that celibacy should be maintained."[10]

"For now, the Church remains firm on the discipline of celibacy," he repeated in another book. "For the time being, I am in favor of maintaining celibacy."[11]

With all the qualifiers about "now" and "the time being," Bergoglio sounded like Murphy-O'Connor, his friend, hinting at future change.

"It is an issue of discipline. . . . It can be changed," Bergoglio finally said of celibacy in his book *On Heaven and Earth*.[12]

In one interview, Bergoglio even casually made a celibacy joke. To illustrate a point about being moderately optimistic about Argentina's future, he told the story of two priests discussing a future council: "One asks the other, 'Will a new Council

9   Catholic Church of England and Wales, "Electing a New Pope," YouTube video, 37:16, February 26, 2013, https://www.youtube.com/watch?v=zkT 3PrsKZCk. See 21:05.

10 Francesca Ambrogetti and Sergio Rubin, *Pope Francis: His Life in His Own Words* (New York: G.P. Putnam's Sons, 2010), 114, Kindle.

11 Jorge Mario Bergoglio and Abraham Skorka, *On Heaven and Earth*, trans. Alejandro Bermudez and Howard Goodman (New York: Image Books, 2013), 48, Kindle.

12 Bergoglio and Skorka, *On Heaven and Earth*, 49.

abolish compulsory celibacy?' The other replies, 'It would seem so.' And the first one says, 'Oh, well, we won't see it, but our children will.'"[13]

By 2014, the groundwork was already being laid for a shift. That year, Murphy-O'Connor told the BBC, "If I were a bishop of a diocese that had a very small number of priests . . . I would ask permission, I think, of Rome to ordain suitable married men."[14] Meanwhile, Pope Francis met with Bishop Erwin Kräutler, a proponent of ordaining married men and women. As they discussed "courageous" proposals, Pope Francis brought up the work of Bishop Fritz Lobinger—an advocate of ordaining married elders, male and female.[15]

In late 2015, vaticanista Sandro Magister confirmed the plan for a new synod on the priestly ordination of married men—tracing the idea back to Martini's 1999 "dream" speech. As Magister explained, since the family synods had already addressed Martini's themes of "sexuality" and "the discipline of marriage," next came the issue of the "deficit of ordained ministers."[16]

Then in 2016, Pope Francis set up a commission to study the possibility of installing a female diaconate.

13   Ambrogetti and Rubin, *Pope Francis*, 229.

14   Liz Dodd, "Cardinal Cormac Murphy-O'Connor Says He Would Ordain Married Men," *The Tablet*, October 3, 2014, https://www.thetablet.co.uk /news/1236/cardinal-cormac-murphy-o-connor-says-he-would-ordain -married-men-.

15   Sandro Magister, "The Conclusions of the Synod For the Amazon Were Already In the Pope's Mind Five Years Ago," *L'Espresso*, October 25, 2019, http://magister.blogautore.espresso.repubblica.it/2019/10/25/the-conclu sions-of-the-synod-for-the-amazon-were-already-in-the-pope%e2%80 %99s-mind-five-years-ago/.

16   Sandro Magister, "The Next Synod Is Already in the Works. On Married Priests," *L'Espresso*, December 9, 2015, http://chiesa.espresso.repubblica .it/articolo/1351189bdc4.html?eng=y.

"Time is the adversary," said Murphy-O'Connor in 2016 regarding women's role in the Church. He said he discussed the issue with Pope Francis. "He's thinking about it," Murphy-O'Connor said. "I think the role of women will increase. . . . I don't think there will be women priests in our time, anyway. Maybe women deacons, possibly."[17]

For in St. Gallen, the mafia had discussed female deacons too. This diaconate, says Danneels's biography, represented a crucial step toward greater openness to women's ordination.[18]

As a 2019 synod on the Amazon approached, Cardinal Walter Brandmüller warned of the plot to install two "cherished projects that heretofore have never been implemented: namely, the abolition of priestly celibacy and the introduction of a female priesthood—beginning with female deacons."[19]

In 2015, Brandmüller had prophetically sketched the full revolutionary arc. "Communion for the divorced and 'remarried' [comes] first," he said. "Then abolition of priestly celibacy, second. Priesthood for women is the ultimate aim, and lastly unification with the Protestants. Then we will have a national German church, independent from Rome. Finally, together with all the Protestants."[20]

17 Cormac Murphy-O'Connor, "Popes I've Known," YouTube video, 1:03:38, February 29, 2016, https://www.youtube.com/watch?v=2BOh0sOFZFI&t=1 879s. See 54:50.

18 Jürgen Mettepenningen and Karim Schelkens, *Godfried Danneels: Biographie* (Antwerpen: Uitgeverij Polis, 2015), 455–456, https://pure.uvt.nl /ws/portalfiles/portal/28312169/Danneels_Polis_FR.pdf.

19 Maike Hickson, "Cardinal Critiques Amazon Synod Working Doc as 'Heretical...Apostasy,' Urges Bishops to 'Reject' It," LifeSiteNews, June 27, 2019, https://www.lifesitenews.com/news/cardinal-critiques-amazon -synod-working-doc-as-heretical-apostasy-urges-bishops-to-reject-it.

20 Edward Pentin, *The Rigging of a Vatican Synod?* (San Francisco: Ignatius Press, 2015), loc. 1714 of 3138, Kindle.

* * *

"Do you think there could be the possibility of a schism because now some people criticize [Pope Francis] for having opened a Pandora's box by calling a synod on the family?" vaticanista Gerard O'Connell asked Murphy-O'Connor early in Francis's revolution.

"No!" the cardinal replied. He said that the future Pope Paul VI, as a cardinal, had said that Pope John XXIII did not know what a can of worms, or Pandora's box, he had opened by calling the Second Vatican Council. Then Murphy-O'Connor said, "So too, I think, when the cardinals elected Bergoglio they did not know what a Pandora's box they were opening, they did not know what a steely character he was, they did not know that he was a Jesuit in very deep ways, they did not know who they were electing."[21]

Pandora's box. It was an ancient symbol for a series of ruinous escapes. And now Murphy-O'Connor embraced it as the caption for the revolutionary process culminating in Francis's pontificate.

Murphy-O'Connor liked to argue that Vatican II's meaning lay in a triumvirate of topics: collegiality, subsidiarity, and synodality. Collegiality meant "the bishops are to rule the Church with the pope," he said. Synodality meant "the synod of bishops would have practical authority," leading to concrete implementation. Subsidiarity meant local churches would be given "more authority."[22]

---

21 Gerard O'Connell, "Murphy-O'Connor: Francis is Open, Honest and Made People Feel Free," *La Stampa*, March 13, 2014, https://www.lastam pa.it/vatican-insider/en/2014/03/13/news/murphy-o-connor-francis-is -open-honest-and-made-people-feel-free-1.35777212.

22 Cormac Murphy-O'Connor, *From the Vision of Pope John XXIII to the Era of Pope Francis* (Redemptorist, 2017). See 45:26.

Pope Francis's "biggest problem," Murphy-O'Connor said, was that he had not fully implemented these principles.[23]

Collegiality, synodality, subsidiarity. Murphy-O'Connor made the slogans sound harmless and bureaucratic enough. But author Ross Douthat saw that the mafia's coded language stood for a dangerous "doctrinal decentralization." By it, "the Vatican would simply step back from certain debates"—launching a free-for-all on everything from divorce to Marxism. That was the logical extension of Kasper's old debate with Ratzinger over the authority of local churches.[24]

For the St. Gallen mafia wanted, in the spirit of postmodernity, to enshrine and celebrate fragmentation and division. They wanted to allow areas such as Germany to embrace the Kasper proposal while Amazonia took up the ordination of married men and deaconesses.

Lyrically, Kasper and Francis spoke of a polyhedron. "If we think of it as a precious stone, [the polyhedron] reflects the light which falls upon it in a wonderfully variegated way," said Kasper in his glowing book on Martin Luther.[25]

Vaticanista Sandro Magister speaks less poetically. "[For Pope Francis], the Church must be made precisely like this: 'polyhedral,' with many sides. In plainer words: in pieces," he says.[26]

The month before the Amazon synod, talk of schism was running loose.

---

23   Murphy-O'Connor, "Popes I've Known." See 51:12.

24   Ross Douthat, *To Change the Church: Pope Francis and the Future of Catholicism* (New York: Simon & Schuster, 2018), 47–48, Kindle.

25   Walter Kasper, *Martin Luther: An Ecumenical Perspective*, trans. William Madges (New York: Paulist Press, 2016), loc. 551 of 655, Kindle.

26   Sandro Magister, "Church Alarm at Full Blast. But Francis is Letting It Sound in Vain," *L'Espresso*, May 11, 2018, http://magister.blogautore.esp resso.repubblica.it/2018/05/11/church-alarm-at-full-blast-but-francis-is -letting-it-sound-in-vain/.

"On the plane to Maputo, you acknowledged being under attack by a sector of the American Church," a reporter from *The New York Times* said to Pope Francis. "Evidently, there are strong criticisms, and there are even some cardinals and bishops, TV [stations], Catholics, American web sites—many criticisms. Even some very close allies have spoken of a plot against you. . . . Are you afraid of a schism in the American Church and if yes, is there something that you could do, dialogue to help avoid it?"

"In the Church there [have been] many schisms," Francis ultimately answered. He spoke of those who criticized Vatican I and Vatican II.

"I don't fear schisms," he said. He prayed they would not exist. "I pray that there are no schisms. But I am not afraid," he repeated later.[27]

And as he spoke, it was hard not to feel the weight of something historian Roberto de Mattei had previously said:

> I have the impression that the ecclesiastical powers and powers outside the Church that worked for the election of Pope Bergoglio are not satisfied with the results of his pontificate. From their point of view, there have been many words but few practical results. Those who sponsor Pope Francis are ready to abandon him if radical change does not take place. It seems he is being given one last chance to revolutionize the Church in the Amazon Synod this coming October. . . .
>
> It seems to me that the announcement made by the German Bishops' Conference by its president, Cardinal Marx, that they will convoke a local synod that will make

---

27 "Full Text of Pope Francis' In-Flight Press Conference from Madagascar," *Catholic News Agency*, September 11, 2019, https://www.catholicnewsagency.com/news/full-text-of-pope-francis-in-flight-press-conference-from-madagascar-82402.

binding decisions about sexual morality, priestly celibacy, and the reduction of clerical power, should be understood as an ultimatum. . . . They seem to be saying that if the pope does not cross the Rubicon, they will cross it themselves. In both cases we would find ourselves facing a declared schism.[28]

On the eve of the Amazon synod, de Mattei added that revolutions historically have long incubation periods. He said that the current Church revolution had been simmering for some sixty years, since the time of Vatican II, and now it was possible that all would "explode very, very rapidly."[29]

*　*　*

Murphy-O'Connor did not live to see the Amazon synod. He died in 2017, a year before Vatican experts Marco Tosatti and Maike Hickson reported the bombshell claim that, a few months after his election, Pope Francis had blocked an investigation of Murphy-O'Connor for alleged sexual abuse.[30] But the spirit of St. Gallen was still there for the synod as the lid to Pandora's box lifted further up and an ominous procession leapt out.

In the Vatican gardens, with Pope Francis watching, a group led by a female native encircled a mandala and bowed down before a *Pachamama* idol.

---

28   Roberto de Mattei, *Love for the Papacy & Filial Resistance to the Pope in the History of the Church* (Brooklyn, NY: Angelico Press, 2019), 202–203.

29   See Julia Meloni, "The Amazon Synod Has Begun, and Pandora's Box Is Opened," *Crisis Magazine*, October 10, 2019, https://www.crisismagazine.com/2019/the-amazon-synod-has-begun-pandoras-box-is-opened.

30   See Maike Hickson, "Source: Pope Blocked Investigation of Abuse Allegations Against Cardinal Who Helped Elect Him," LifeSiteNews, September 24, 2018, https://www.lifesitenews.com/blogs/source-pope-blocked-investigation-of-abuse-allegations-against-cardinal-who; and Marco Tosatti, *Neovatican Gallery* (Italy: Edizioni Radio Spada, 2021), 49–55.

In the synod hall, a final document endorsed the priestly ordination of married deacons and further study of a female diaconate.[31]

Outside the synod, Fr. Thomas Weinandy warned of possible "internal papal schism." He pointed out that Pope Francis remained the "ultimate protector" of German leaders who promote "ambiguous teaching and pastoral practice . . . in accord with Francis's own." There was thus the danger that the pope, even as pope, would "effectively be the leader of a segment of the Church that through its doctrine, moral teaching, and ecclesial structure, is for all practical purposes schismatic."

"This," said Weinandy, "is the real schism that is in our midst and must be faced, but I do not believe Pope Francis is in any way afraid of this schism. As long as he is in control, he will, I fear, welcome it, for he sees the schismatic element as the new 'paradigm' for the future Church."[32]

Things were falling apart.

But a few months after the synod, a cry rose up from Benedict.

* * *

"Save us, Lord, for we are perishing!"

The cry swelled up from Benedict in his 2020 book *From the Depths of Our Hearts*, written with Cardinal Robert Sarah. "The Lord is asleep while the storm is unleashed. He seems to abandon us to the waves of doubt and error. We are tempted to

31 Edward Pentin, "Three Key Paragraphs of Amazon Synod's Final Document," *The National Catholic Register*, October 26, 2019, https://www.ncregister.com/blog/three-key-paragraphs-of-amazon-synod-s-final-document.

32 Thomas Weinandy, "Pope Francis and Schism," *The Catholic Thing*, October 8, 2019, https://www.thecatholicthing.org/2019/10/08/pope-francis-and-schism/.

2

2

2

2

lose confidence. On every side, the waves of relativism are submerging the barque of the Church," they said.[33]

Just before the 2005 conclave, Ratzinger had spoken against the winds of the dictatorship of relativism. Then, as Pope Benedict XVI, he had repeatedly stressed celibacy's mysterious power against the storm.[34]

Now, in their 2020 book, Benedict and Sarah cried:

It is urgent and necessary for everyone . . . to stop letting themselves be intimidated by the wrong-headed pleas, the theatrical productions, the diabolical lies, and the fashionable errors that try to devalue down priestly celibacy.

It is urgent and necessary for everyone . . . to take a fresh look with the eyes of faith at the Church and at priestly celibacy, which protects her mystery.

This fresh look will be the best rampart against the spirit of division, against the spirit of politics, but also against the spirit of indifference and relativism.[35]

33 Benedict XVI and Robert Sarah, *From the Depths of Our Hearts: Priesthood, Celibacy, and the Crisis of the Catholic Church*, trans. Michael Miller (San Francisco: Ignatius Press, 2020), 12–13, Kindle.

34 See Sandro Magister, "'Why They Are Attacking Me.' Autobiography of a Pontificate," *L'Espresso*, September 3, 2010, https://chiesa.espresso.repubblica.it/articolo/1344604bdc4.html.

35 Benedict XVI and Sarah, *From the Depths*, 82.

15

Patience

The ticking followed Francis still, persisting in asking whether he would arrive on time. Early on in his pontificate, Francis seemed rushed, stretched. He spoke almost eerily about it.

"Four or five years," he told a Mexican broadcaster when asked about how long he thought his pontificate would last. "I do not know, even two or three. Two have already passed."

"It is a somewhat vague sensation," he added, cryptically. "Maybe it's like the psychology of the gambler who convinces himself he will lose, so he won't be disappointed and if he wins, is happy. I do not know."[1]

Later that year, Austen Ivereigh, Murphy-O'Connor's former spokesman, referenced those remarks to reveal the existence of Pope Francis's "five-year plan."

"What was interesting was that he said to Mexican television—it was about a year ago now—that he believed that he would have a short papacy, he thought, of about five years," said

1 "Pope Francis on His Pontificate to Date," Vatican Radio, March 13, 2015, www.archivioradiovaticana.va/storico/2015/03/13/pope_francis_on_his _pontificate_to_date/en-1129074.

Ivereigh of Francis. "What I'm now hearing, though, from people close to him, is that he now believes he's going to need seven
years to achieve his five-year plan."[2]

Which placed the plan's completion date at 2020.

In his 2009 interview with Eugenio Scalfari, Martini clearly
explained, in order, the most important topics for the revolution: divorce, priestly celibacy, and the relationship between the
Church's hierarchy and politics.

In his 1999 "dream" speech, Martini started with celibacy,
proceeded to issues of sexuality and marriage, and ended with
the relationship between civil law and moral law.

Other mafia members made clear what the last goal
included.

Regarding same-sex "marriage," Danneels said shortly after
Francis's election that "insofar as it is legal," the Church "does
not have a say."[3]

Addressing the same issue in Ireland, Kasper likewise said,
"A democratic state has the duty to respect the will of the people; and it seems clear that, if the majority of the people wants
such homosexual unions, the state has a duty to recognize such
rights."[4]

---

2   Current News, "Pope Francis to Resign in 2020?" YouTube video, 5:25,
     December 7, 2015, https://www.youtube.com/watch?v=zuN2ZVApdIc&
     t=10s. See 0:35. While Ivereigh then speculated about a possible papal
     abdication at that time, he later clarified that he did not think Francis
     would resign while Benedict lived. See Austen Ivereigh, *Wounded Shep-
     herd: Pope Francis and His Struggle to Convert the Catholic Church* (New
     York: Henry Holt, 2019), 332, Kindle.

3   "Belgium's Cardinal Danneels Okays Same-Sex Unions," *La Stampa*, June
     7, 2013, https://www.lastampa.it/vatican-insider/en/2013/06/07/news
     /belgium-s-cardinal-danneels-okays-same-sex-unions-1.36081745.

4   Maike Hickson, "Cardinal Kasper Defends Ireland's Gay 'Marriage' De-
     cision," LifeSiteNews, May 29, 2015, https://www.lifesitenews.com/news
     /gay-unions-now-central-to-synod-agenda-after-irish-vote-cardinal-ka
     sper.

* * *

Francis did not like to be tardy for things. Describing the "black plastic watch" on his right wrist at the time of the 2013 conclave, biographer Elisabetta Piqué says that he "is very punctual, he doesn't like being late."[5]

But even Francis, the executive, understood the power of patience.

"Traveling with patience," he said as a cardinal, "is knowing that what matures is time. Traveling with patience is allowing time to rule and shape our lives."[6]

In *Evangelii Gaudium*, Pope Francis put it this way: "Time is greater than space. This principle enables us to work slowly but surely, without being obsessed with immediate results. It helps us patiently to endure difficult and adverse situations, or inevitable changes in our plans. It invites us to accept the tension between fullness and limitation, and to give a priority to time. Giving priority to time means being concerned about initiating processes rather than possessing spaces."[7]

"Time is greater than space." It sounded so academic, so esoteric, but it could have been the mantra for Bergoglio's life.

Back when Bergoglio was a young Jesuit in Argentina, he had a dream. "I was in the seminary," he later recalled to an interviewer. "I had a very severe encounter with suffering: A piece of my lung was removed due to three cysts. This very intense experience colors my memory of the time you ask me

---

5   Elisabetta Piqué, *Pope Francis: Life and Revolution: A Biography of Jorge Bergoglio* (Chicago: Loyola Press, 2014), 4, Kindle.

6   Francesca Ambrogetti and Sergio Rubin, *Pope Francis: His Life in His Own Words* (New York: G.P. Putnam's Sons, 2010), 72, Kindle.

7   Pope Francis, *Evangelii Gaudium*, Vatican website, http://www.vatican .va/content/francesco/en/apost_exhortations/documents/papa-frances co_esortazione-ap_20131124_evangelii-gaudium.html, 222–223.

to recall, but there is one very intimate thing I remember well: I was full of hopes and dreams."[8]

As Austen Ivereigh recounts, a couple of years after his lung operation, Bergoglio and his fellow Jesuit novices were visited by Fr. Pedro Arrupe, the then provincial in Japan for the Jesuits. When Arrupe told the novices the gripping history of the Jesuits in east Asia, Bergoglio was arrested.[9]

He asked to be considered for missionary work in Japan. Arrupe told him to ask the superior general after completing more studies. Later, when Arrupe himself rose to head the Jesuits, Bergoglio asked about Japan and Arrupe said no—because of Bergoglio's lung.[10]

So Bergoglio traveled in patience. He threw himself into teaching high school literature. One day, the progressive Jesuit provincial of the Argentine region was ousted under conservative pressure and Bergoglio suddenly became provincial at an exceptionally young age. At the Jesuits' 1974 General Congregation, Bergoglio met Martini,[11] who gave a speech about justice that Bergoglio would remember even many years later.[12]

In those days, Martini and Bergoglio seemed to be two divergent stars. While Martini was aligning himself with the progressive Jesuit program of Arrupe, Bergoglio was earning a reputation for being "ultraconservative." According to author Paul Vallely and witnesses from this period, Bergoglio donned a cassock, assigned old Latin textbooks, replaced post-conciliar

---

8   Pope Francis, *God is Young* (New York: Random House, 2018), 6, Kindle.

9   Austen Ivereigh, *The Great Reformer: Francis and the Making of a Radical Pope* (New York: Henry Holt & Co., 2014), 67, Kindle.

10   Ivereigh, *The Great Reformer*, 67, 76.

11   Ivereigh, *The Great Reformer*, 262.

12   Thomas C. Fox, "Francis Hails Late Cardinal Carlo Martini," *The National Catholic Reporter*, September 2, 2013, https://www.ncronline.org/blo gs/francis-chronicles/francis-hails-late-cardinal-carlo-martini.

songs with Gregorian plainchant, encouraged students to touch statues, replaced progressive teachers with conservatives, and forbade the teaching of liberation theology.[13]

What no one realized, however, was that Bergoglio was traveling in patience toward Martini's position.

Bergoglio began his episcopal career as a conservative—and then, as his biographers stress, reconnected with Martini in 2001. Something happened in this period. Increasingly, as a cardinal, Bergoglio faced accusations "of not being orthodox enough," says Piqué. "Bergoglio is accused of not defending doctrine, of making pastoral gestures that are too daring, and of not arguing publicly with greater determination with the Argentine government of the time."[14]

"They reproached him for not being demanding enough with the faithful, for not showing clearly his identity as priest, for not preaching enough on questions of sexual morality," says Archbishop Víctor Manuel Fernández, Bergoglio's ghostwriter. "He knew how to suffer in silence," Fernández adds. "Bergoglio kept quiet and bided his time."[15]

Then Bergoglio traveled in patience all the way to the papacy.

* * *

Patience. In *The Great Reformer*, Ivereigh points out that one of Francis's "lodestars" was the Vatican II theologian Yves Congar.[16] Congar, like Francis, was obsessed with time. Congar was obsessed with a "spirit of intentional patience," by which one does not "rush immediately or quickly to conclusions" but

13   Paul Vallely, *Pope Francis: The Struggle for the Soul of Catholicism* (London: Bloomsbury, 2015), loc. 1255 of 11235, Kindle.

14   Piqué, *Pope Francis*, 125–126.

15   Piqué, *Pope Francis*, 131–133.

16   Ivereigh, *The Great Reformer*, prologue.

rather recognizes "that delays are needed to bring things to maturity."[17]

"In any reform movement, impatience threatens to ruin everything," Congar said. "The innovator, whose reform turns into schism, lacks patience. He does not respect the slowness either of God or of the church, or the delays that come into everyone's life. He moves with a kind of inflexible and exasperated logic toward 'all or nothing' solutions."[18]

And so Congar set a very important condition for changing the Church without inducing schism: "having patience with delays." Congar "proposed to change the Church from within, through 'a reform without schism,'" says historian Roberto de Mattei. As Congar himself put it, "We don't need to create *another church*. What we need to some degree is a church that is *other*."[19]

"Luther was an impatient reformer," Congar said. Luther did not know how to hold back "when tempted by simple, abrupt solutions or by extremes of 'all or nothing.'"[20] So at the Second Vatican Council, Congar tried to make sure that the revolutionaries did not show the impatience of Luther. As he put it in his diary, "As for me, I believe profoundly in time-lags, in the necessary stages."[21]

It was what the mafia's members wanted too, like classic Modernists: to change the Church from within, patiently, without outright schism.

17 Yves Congar, *True and False Reform in the Church*, trans. Paul Philibert (Collegeville, MN: Liturgical Press, 2011), 343–344, Kindle.
18 Congar, *True and False Reform*, 265.
19 Roberto de Mattei, *The Second Vatican Council: An Unwritten Story* (Fitzwilliam, NH: Loreto Publications, 2013), loc. 2821 of 16572, Kindle.
20 Congar, *True and False Reform*, 269.
21 Yves Congar, *My Journal of the Council* (South Africa: ATF Press, 2012), 370.

In 1993, Martini cited the example of women priests. He admitted that a sudden change on the issue would risk schism, and "the pope has to be concerned with keeping his huge flock with all its different opinions together." Still, he continued, "As for the issue itself, I think we should come to it little by little, to gradual solutions that will satisfy not only the most progressive but also the majority, while remaining true to tradition and also within the bounds of common sense. That's my opinion. But I can foresee decades of struggle ahead."

Then, implying a radical change after those "decades of struggle," he quipped in 1993, "When people ask me, and it's usually Americans, 'Will we have women priests?' I answer: 'Not in this millennium!'"[22]

Some have speculated that this interview may have helped push Pope John Paul II to release the 1994 document *Sacerdotalis Ordinatio*, which affirmed that "the Church has no authority whatsoever to confer priestly ordination on women." Yet just three days after that document's release, Martini was back to his subversive ways, telling a Eucharistic Congress in Siena, "The Pope has said nothing about the ordination of women to the diaconate." Asserting the presence of a female diaconate in the past, he said, "I think that a certain space remains open."[23]

Ultimately, Martini hailed Martin Luther as a "great reformer" but said, in *Night Conversations*, "I have a problem with the fact that he makes a separate system out of necessary reforms and ideals."[24]

Working slowly within the Church was the mafia's way.

22　Peter Hebblethwaite, *The Next Pope* (San Francisco: Harper, 1995), 162.
23　Hebblethwaite, *The Next Pope*, 167.
24　Carlo Maria Martini and Georg Sporschill, *Night Conversations with Cardinal Martini*, trans. Lorna Henry (New York: Paulist Press, 2012), 86, NOOK.

* * *

When Pope Francis released his post-synodal exhortation *Querida Amazonia* in February 2020, the text's quiet aura of patience calmed many.

After the clamor of the Amazon synod, embodied by its *Pachamama* idols, *Querida Amazonia* seemed disarmingly reticent, restrained. The text quietly dropped the thorny issue of the ordination of married men—or so it seemed.

Querida Amazonia is "very clever," says Cardinal Oswald Gracias, one of the advisors in Francis's council of cardinals. In the text, says Gracias, Francis is "endorsing the final document" of the Amazon synod—which itself endorses the ordination of married men and further study of the female diaconate.[25]

"By endorsing the [final] document he leaves [the issue of the ordination of married men] open," Gracias says. Regarding the role of women in the Church, Gracias says the pope's "mind is open," but "there are pressures." "There are people who do not want any change," says the cardinal. "There are people who want overnight changes. But he's got to carry everybody with him."[26]

"The pope speaks of synodality, where we take everyone along with us," Gracias continues. "And then, if necessary, we go slower than we would like to go because of that."[27]

"Go slower." It was one of the interpretive keys to the Francis pontificate. The pope frequently had to move more slowly, more patiently to carry everyone in the boat.

25   Joshua McElwee, "Cardinal Gracias: Church Must 'Shed Prejudice' Against Women's Leadership," *The National Catholic Reporter*, February 24, 2020, https://www.ncronline.org/news/people/cardinal-gracias-church-must -shed-prejudice-against-womens-leadership?clickSource=email.

26   McElwee, "Cardinal Gracias: Church Must 'Shed Prejudice.'"

27   McElwee, "Cardinal Gracias: Church Must 'Shed Prejudice.'"

Francis wanted—according to his ghostwriter—to "go slow" in order to make his changes "irreversible." "If you go slowly it's more difficult to turn things back," said the advisor.[28]

And so Francis carefully turned to synodality—the key component of Martini's 1999 "dream."

"Synods are consultative bodies, and they usually leave the difficult decisions to the pope," says a writer for *The National Catholic Reporter*. "But Francis wants us to move away from that monarchical model. . . . You can't achieve synodality if you continually look to the pope to make the tough calls. Instead of the synod being a consultative body that helps the pope form his own judgment, here he is giving the outcome of the synod's deliberations its own standing and status."[29]

Which meant that *Querida Amazonia* was another calculated chess move against the king, another attempt to downgrade the monarchical papacy via synodality.

But it was a move so quiet that you almost forgot the intelligence sitting across from you, hand on the pawn, patiently holding an endgame in mind.

* * *

Patience. The revolutionaries had to move patiently enough to avoid an outright schism. And yet in 2019, during his Christmas address to the Curia, Pope Francis urged "courage" in changing the Church.

---

28   John-Henry Westen and Maike Hickson, "One of the Pope's Closest Advisors: How Pope Francis is Changing the Church," LifeSiteNews, June 4, 2015, https://www.lifesitenews.com/news/one-of-popes-closest-advisors-how-pope-francis-is-changing-the-church.

29   Michael Sean Winters, "'Querida Amazonia' Shows How Francis is Looking for Deeper Change," *The National Catholic Reporter*, February 13, 2020, https://www.ncronline.org/news/opinion/distinctly-catholic/querida-amazonia-shows-how-francis-looking-deeper-change.

"Cardinal Martini, in his last interview, a few days before his death, said something that should make us think," said Pope Francis. Then he quoted, at full strength, some startling last words of Martini: "The Church is two hundred years behind the times. Why is she not shaken up? Are we afraid? Fear, instead of courage?"[30]

Francis started out quietly, but as he read Martini's last testament, his hands became animated. His facial expression grew almost stark as he channeled the man who had prepared the way for him.

"Faith, confidence, courage," Francis said, gesturing, his eyes squinting a bit. Then Francis lowered his head downward and scanned the room, as if searching for the men who would seize Martini's dream. "Only love conquers weariness," he said.[31]

"The Church is two hundred years behind." As historian Roberto de Mattei points out, "Martini's idea is that the Church is two centuries behind the times because it has not had its French Revolution."[32] Martini was crying for a parallel upheaval, in lockstep with the world—and so in 2012, as the revolutionary movement for same-sex unions swept the globe, Martini spoke out.

"I disagree with the positions of those in the Church that take issue with civil unions," Martini wrote in *Credere e Conoscere*. "It is not bad, instead of casual sex between men, that two people have a certain stability."[33]

30   "Address of His Holiness Pope Francis," Vatican website, December 21, 2019, https://www.vatican.va/content/francesco/en/speeches/2019/december/documents/papa-francesco_20191221_curia-romana.html.

31   Vatican News, "Pope Francis—Audience Roman Curia 2019-12-21," YouTube video, 39:50, https://www.youtube.com/watch?v=mHm8QQymCps&t=1924s. See 34:18.

32   Roberto de Mattei, "In Memoriam: The French Historian and the Italian Philosopher," *Rorate Caeli* (blog), January 8, 2020, https://rorate-caeli.blogspot.com/2020/01/de-mattei-in-memoriam-french-historian.html.

33   John-Henry Westen, "Cardinal Martini and the False Theology Pro-

That same year, in 2012, the Congregation for the Doctrine of the Faith reprinted Ratzinger's 1986 instruction on the topic of homosexuality. As vaticanista Sandro Magister puts it, "The 1986 letter warns that 'there is an effort in some countries to manipulate the Church by gaining the often well-intentioned support of her pastors with a view to changing civil-statutes and laws,' in such a way as to make it conform to 'pressure groups.'"[34]

And yet Ratzinger's words from 1986 could not stop the relentless clock of revolution.

Around 2000, the mafia decided to prioritize the topic of homosexuality.[35] A decade later, in 2010, Bergoglio encouraged his fellow Argentine bishops to support legislation for same-sex civil unions—directly flouting Ratzinger's 2003 instruction to offer emphatic opposition to legal recognition of homosexual unions of any kind.[36] A decade later, in 2020, Pope Francis said, referencing same-sex couples, "What we have to create is a civil union law. That way they are legally covered. I stood up for that."[37]

And with that, you saw a hand sweep across the chessboard, heard a sound at the mantelpiece, and understood why the revolutionaries traveled in patience.

moting Homosexuality," LifeSiteNews, March 27, 2012, https://www.lifesitenews.com/opinion/cardinal-martini-and-the-false-theology-promoting-homosexuality.

34 Sandro Magister, "Vatican Diary / That Sin of Sodom Which Cries Out to Heaven," L'Espresso, May 18, 2012, http://chiesa.espresso.repubblica.it/articolo/1350247bdc4.html.

35 Jürgen Mettepenningen and Karim Schelkens, Godfried Danneels: Biographie (Antwerpen: Uitgeverij Polis, 2015), 451, https://pure.uvt.nl/ws/portalfiles/portal/28312169/Danneels_Polis_FR.pdf.

36 Ivereigh, The Great Reformer, 313.

37 "Pope Francis Calls for Civil Union Law for Same-Sex Couples, in Shift From Vatican Stance," Catholic News Agency, October 21, 2020, https://www.catholicnewsagency.com/news/pope-francis-calls-for-civil-union-law-for-same-sex-couples-in-shift-from-vatican-stance-12462.

16

Time

Time, the mysterious cardinal of *Confession d'un Cardinal*
once said, is "our first master." You had to arrive on time—
neither too early nor too late. And if you made it on time,
whether by "chance" or by "calculation," you seized control of
your destiny.[1]

One day in 2005, the mysterious cardinal announced some
"appointment with history" that the Church needed to keep.
The Church had to go "global," had to work with institutions
to fight merciless market logic, had to bring "tenderness" to the
world in this specific, fleeting window of time.[2]

In his 2011 book *L'Espérance du Cardinal*, the mysterious cardinal further spoke of St. Francis of Assisi, nature, and
the universal "dream" of "fraternity." In a flight of reverie, the
unnamed cardinal thought of how, after attending the controversial 1986 inter-religious meeting in Assisi, he had stayed
to read St. Bonaventure's *vita* of Francis, and the weather had
turned mild. On very little sleep, the mysterious cardinal

---

1   Olivier Le Gendre, *Confession d'un Cardinal* (Paris: JC Lattès, 2007), 67,
     NOOK.
2   Le Gendre, *Confession d'un Cardinal*, 297–300.

roamed the streets of Assisi—praying, admiring nature, and searching for Francis, bearer of God's "tenderness."[3]

It seemed as if a new Francis had an appointment to keep with the global Left.

Back in his earlier days, Martini had tried to be the one to arrive on time. In the late 1980s, he presided over a major ecumenical gathering on peace, justice, and the care of creation.[4] During his time as archbishop of Milan, he created a special forum in which atheists taught Christians how to save the world.[5] In *Night Conversations*, Martini championed environmentalism,[6] leftism,[7] fraternity,[8] and the need for the Church to bring "cooperative development agencies" into dialogue on condoms.[9]

But like one on a fast train, Martini arrived perpetually early.

Then Benedict XVI's 2013 resignation came—said Kasper—like "lightning from a clear blue sky."[10] With almost cosmic suddenness, Bergoglio took the papal name Francis—and the pope became, in the words of *The Wall Street Journal*, "the leader of

3 Olivier Le Gendre, *L'Espérance du Cardinal* (Paris: JC Lattès, 2011), 141–146, NOOK.

4 For background on this 1989 gathering at Basel, Switzerland, see Aldo Maria Valli, *Storia di un Uomo: Ritratto di Carlo Maria Martini* (Milan: Ancora, 2011), loc. 1853 of 3334, Kindle.

5 Carlo Maria Martini and Georg Sporschill, *Night Conversations with Cardinal Martini*, trans. Lorna Henry (New York: Paulist Press, 2012), 80, NOOK.

6 Martini and Sporschill, *Night Conversations with Cardinal Martini*, 13, 95–96.

7 Martini and Sporschill, *Night Conversations with Cardinal Martini*, 40, 56.

8 Martini and Sporschill, *Night Conversations with Cardinal Martini*, 40.

9 Martini and Sporschill, *Night Conversations with Cardinal Martini*, 73.

10 Walter Kasper, *Pope Francis' Revolution of Tenderness and Love*, trans. William Madges (New York: Paulist Press, 2015), 12, Google Books.

the global Left."[11] Quickly, Pope Francis released an environ-mentalist encyclical, *Laudato Si'*, which called for "one world with a common plan." It eerily echoed the themes of *Confession d'un Cardinal*—speaking many times of the heartless market, nine times of "tenderness," and seven times of "fraternity."[12] With this encyclical and other gestures, Pope Francis helped clinch the acceptance of both the Paris Agreement on climate change and the UN's Sustainable Development Goals—which include coded provisions for "universal access" to contracep-tion and abortion.[13]

"Pope Francis had a huge part to play in that [acceptance of the agreements]. Enormous. *Laudato Si'* was an inspiration," says leftist economist Jeffrey Sachs.[14]

"Pope Francis, as liberals once said of Barack Obama, is the 'one they have been waiting for,'" says journalist George Neumayr.[15]

11 Francis Rocca, "How Pope Francis Became the Leader of the Global Left," *The Wall Street Journal*, December 22, 2016, https://www.wsj.com/articles/how-pope-francis-became-the-leader-of-the-global-left-14824 31940.

12 Pope Francis, *Laudato Si'*, Vatican website, May 24, 2015, http://www.vatican.va/content/francesco/en/encyclicals/documents/papa-francesco_20150524_enciclica-laudato-si.html.

13 See Lianne Laurence, "Catholics Must 'Resist' Pope Francis' Alliance with Pro-abortion United Nations: Catholic Coalition," LifeSiteNews, February 28, 2017, https://www.lifesitenews.com/news/vatican-under-francis-has-betrayed-children-by-supporting-un-pro-abortion-g. As the report points out, "Goals 3 and 5 of the SDGs call for 'universal access to sex-ual and reproductive health and reproductive rights,' terms that pro-life leaders say have been used consistently by the UN for years to push ac-cess to abortion, contraception, and sterilization."

14 Jeffrey Sachs, "Pope Francis and *Laudato Si'*," Villanova University web-site, April 13, 2018, https://www1.villanova.edu/content/dam/villanova/mission/catholic-social-thought/2019-CST-Materials/BW-Sachs%20Talk.pdf.

15 George Neumayr, *The Political Pope: How Pope Francis Is Delighting the*

* * *

They had been waiting for him, dreaming of him, and in the end he had arrived right on time. But had he made it to the appointment with history by chance or by calculation?

In 2005, the mysterious cardinal of *Confession d'un Cardinal* had spoken of keeping sixty-eight-year-old Bergoglio in mind just "in case" Benedict's pontificate did not last long.[16] The mysterious cardinal was obsessed with the issue of aging. What, he wondered, would have happened if John Paul II had died a year later, in 2006, when Ratzinger was seventy-nine instead of seventy-eight? Recalling the unspoken, informal rule against electing cardinals eighty and over, the mysterious cardinal envisaged some "Cardinal X" who could have been elected instead.[17]

But now, the mysterious cardinal said in 2005, Cardinal X would probably become too old for the papacy by the time Benedict's successor was chosen.[18]

In his 2011 follow-up book to *Confession d'un Cardinal*, the mysterious cardinal, who may have been Silvestrini sounded more sanguine. He made it clear that he and some nebulous others ("we") felt that Benedict's successor could carry out their project on regional councils.[19] Later, after lamenting that non-Italian, non-Curial candidates as well as candidates from the global South were underrepresented for the next papal election, the mysterious cardinal pointed something out. He said the election would, in fact, be determined by the personality of the man—and the conclave's timing.[20]

Liberal Left and Abandoning Conservatives (New York: Center Street, 2017), 10, Kindle.

16   Le Gendre, *Confession d'un Cardinal*, 121.

17   Le Gendre, *Confession d'un Cardinal*, 66-67.

18   Le Gendre, *Confession d'un Cardinal*, 67.

19   Le Gendre, *L'Espérance du Cardinal*, 60.

20   Le Gendre, *L'Espérance du Cardinal*, 210.

Time. In 2012, Kasper spoke of a "southerly wind" rising in the Church. "Since 2012, we have been using an image created by Cardinal Walter Kasper: *a southerly wind blows*," theologian Carlos María Galli would later say—treating Kasper's image as a prefigurement of Bergoglio's rise.[21]

And yet by 2012, time was running out for Bergoglio, who would turn seventy-six that December. And it was almost out for Martini, who would die in August.

In January 2012, Martini spoke suggestively about the Church's future to a confidante.

"Your Eminence, one must truly weep over our Church," said the confidante.

"No. This will pass, it will pass!" said Martini.

"It will pass? And Benedict XVI?"

"He too will pass," Martini said. "I saw him in April [of 2011]. I saw a tired old man. I hope that he will resign soon. Then we will be done with the secretary of state and the secretariat of state."

"And afterward, Your Eminence?"

"Afterward there will be a conclave that will choose. Perhaps Scola," said Martini.[22]

In March 2012, Martini and the confidante spoke again.

"I, last year, succeeded in having direct contact with [Pope Benedict] two times," Martini said. Then he related, "In April I

21 See Antonio Spadaro and Carlos María Galli, *For a Missionary Reform of the Church: The La Civiltà Cattolica Seminar* (Mahwah, NJ: Paulist Press, 2017), loc. 882 of 13161, Kindle. See also Walter Kasper, *Chiesa Cattolica: Essenza, Realtà, Missione* (Brescia: Queriniana, 2012), 46. I am grateful to Maike Hickson for pointing this passage out to me.

22 Sandro Magister, "Jesuits Against Focolarini. The Beatification of Chiara Lubich in Doubt," *L'Espresso*, November 8, 2018, http://magister.blogaut ore.espresso.repubblica.it/2018/11/08/jesuits-against-focolarini-the-bea tification-of-chiara-lubich-in-doubt/.

and a few other bishops will go to Switzerland—that way they too will be more free."[23]

As Martini's priest-secretary confirms, in April 2012 Martini indeed went to a meeting of unnamed bishop friends near Switzerland's border with Germany.[24]

* * *

Time. In June 2012, two months after his mysterious meeting in Switzerland, Martini met Benedict for the last time at the World Meeting of Families in Milan.

"The Curia is not going to change; you have no choice but to leave," Martini said to Benedict, looking the pope in the eye, according to Martini's confessor, Fr. Silvano Fausti. "The time [for resignation] is now; nothing can be done here anymore," Martini added.[25]

The way Martini's confessor told the story, Benedict's resignation had been scripted since his pontificate's beginning—because Martini had shifted his votes to Ratzinger at the 2005 conclave to prevent the ascent of a "slippery" Curial figure. "Tomorrow, accept the papacy with my votes," Martini is said to have told Ratzinger in 2005. "You accept, since you have been in the Curia for years; you're intelligent and honest; try and reform the Curia, and if not, you leave."[26]

According to vaticanista Andrea Tornielli, while Fausti's account of what happened at the 2005 conclave is open to

23   Magister, "Jesuits Against Focolarini."
24   Damiano Modena, *Carlo Maria Martini: Il Silenzio della Parola* (Milan: San Paolo, 2013), loc. 490 of 1190, Kindle.
25   "The Original Story: When the Jesuit Cardinal told Pope Benedict XVI He Had to Resign," *Rorate Caeli* (blog), July 24, 2015, https://rorate-caeli.blogspot.com/2015/07/the-original-story-when-jesuit-cardinal.html.
26   "The Original Story," *Rorate Caeli.*

interpretation, there is "no doubt" that Martini told Benedict, in 2012, to resign.[27]

In one of Antonio Socci's books on Benedict XVI, there is a chapter called "Dances with Wolves." It alludes to Benedict's cryptic cry after his election: "Pray for me, that I may not flee for fear of the wolves." The chapter recounts the "open war" against the German pope and narrates how Socci himself reported, in September 2011, that Benedict would potentially resign at age eighty-five—news that, apparently, was already known in Curial circles in the summer of 2011.[28]

And yet what is interesting about the phrase "dances with wolves" is that it is not an image of open war.

It is an image of trustfully befriending something dangerous.

We may never know for certain if, when Martini shifted his votes to Ratzinger and walked arm-in-arm with him during the 2005 conclave, the two entered not into a pact but a certain rapport of trust. We may never know for certain if, years later, Martini used that rapport to assure the pope (just as he had assured his own confidante) that the conservative Scola would probably succeed Benedict if he resigned. We may never know for certain if Martini spoke with Benedict about an abdication already in 2011—leading Martini, in early 2012, to say to his confidante, with a kind of insider's optimism, that he hoped Benedict would resign "soon."

We may never know for certain just how much calculation went into harnessing the southerly wind that would sweep Bergoglio, the Martini pope, into Benedict's place. But

27   Andrea Tornielli, "Martini: Benedict XVI's Resignation and the 2005 Conclave," *La Stampa*, July 18, 2015, https://www.lastampa.it/vatican-in sider/en/2015/07/18/news/martini-benedict-xvi-s-resignation-and-the -2005-conclave-1.35243041.

28   Antonio Socci, *Non è Francesco. La Chiesa Nella Grande Tempesta* (Milan: Mondadori, 2015), 57-58.

as Benedict announced his abdication on February 11, 2013 and lightning struck St. Peter's twice, an "acceleration of time" occurred.[29]

Motus in fine velocior—motion accelerates toward the end. Time passes more swiftly at a period's close—and "we are living," says historian Roberto de Mattei, "through an historical hour which is not necessarily the end of times, but certainly the end of a civilization and the termination of an epoch in the life of the Church."[30]

For a clock wound up with its inexorable ticking and the revolutionaries had to hurry. For some dreams, like Martini's, are, finally, as fleeting as lightning, destined to evanesce while somewhere in the Sistine Chapel the Christ of *The Last Judgment* gazes on.

---

29   Roberto de Mattei, "'Motus in Fine Velocior'—The Crisis is Gathering Speed," *Rorate Caeli* (blog), October 10, 2019, https://rorate-caeli.blogsp ot.com/2019/10/motus-in-fine-velocior-crisis-is.html.

30   De Mattei, "'Motus in Fine Velocior.'"

Bibliography

Allen, John, Jr., *The Rise of Benedict XVI: The Inside Story of How the Pope Was Elected and Where He Will Take the Church*. New York: Doubleday, 2007.

Ambrogetti, Francesca and Sergio Rubin. *Pope Francis: His Life in His Own Words*. New York: G.P. Putnam's Sons, 2010.

Badde, Paul. *Benedict Up Close: The Inside Story of Eight Dramatic Years*. Irondale, AL: EWTN, 2017.

Benedict XVI and Peter Seewald. *Last Testament: In His Own Words*. Translated by Jacob Phillips. London: Bloomsbury, 2016.

Benedict XVI and Peter Seewald. *Light of the World: The Pope, the Church, and the Signs of the Times*. Translated by Michael Miller and Adrian Walker. San Francisco: Ignatius Press, 2010.

Benedict XVI and Robert Sarah. *From the Depths of Our Hearts: Priesthood, Celibacy, and the Crisis of the Catholic Church*. Translated by Michael Miller. San Francisco: Ignatius Press, 2020.

Bergoglio, Jorge Mario and Abraham Skorka. *On Heaven and Earth*. Translated by Alejandro Bermudez and Howard Goodman. New York: Image Books, 2013.

Colberg, Kristin M. and Robert A. Krieg, eds. *The Theology of Cardinal Walter Kasper: Speaking Truth in Love.* Collegeville, MN: Liturgical Press, 2010.

Colonna, Marcantonio [Henry Sire]. *The Dictator Pope: The Inside Story of the Francis Papacy.* Washington, DC: Regnery, 2017.

Congar, Yves. *My Journal of the Council.* South Africa: ATF Press, 2012.

Congar, Yves. *True and False Reform in the Church.* Translated by Paul Philibert. Collegeville, MN: Liturgical Press, 2011.

Conway, Eamonn. "Rahner's 'Tough Love' for the Church: Structural Change as Task and Opportunity." In *Karl Rahner: Theologian for the Twenty-First Century.* Edited by Padraic Conway and Fainche Ryan. Oxford: Peter Lang, 2010.

Costa, Giacomo. *Il Discernimento.* Milan: Edizioni San Paolo, 2018.

Curran, Charles and Julie Hanlon Rubio, eds. *Marriage: Readings in Moral Theology No. 15.* New York: Paulist Press, 2009.

Danneels, Godfried. *Confidences d'un Cardinal.* Bruxelles: Racine, 2009.

Danneels, Godfried. *Words of Life: Volume 1.* Translated by Matthew J. O'Connell. Kansas City, MO: Sheed & Ward, 1991.

De Mattei, Roberto. *Love for the Papacy & Filial Resistance to the Pope in the History of the Church.* Brooklyn, NY: Angelico Press, 2019.

De Mattei, Roberto. *The Second Vatican Council: An Unwritten Story.* Fitzwilliam, NH: Loreto Publications, 2013.

Diat, Nicolas. *L'Homme Qui Ne Voulait Pas Être Pape: Histoire Secrète d'un Règne.* Paris: Albin Michel, 2014.

Douthat, Ross. *To Change the Church: Pope Francis and the Future of Catholicism.* New York: Simon & Schuster, 2018.

Facchini, Maris Martini. *L'Infanzia di un Cardinale: Mio Fratello Carlo Maria. Ricordi e Immagini di Vita Familiare.* Milan: Ancora, 2018.

Fontana, Stefano. *La Nuova Chiesa di Karl Rahner: Il Teologo che ha Insegnato ad Arrendersi al Mondo.* Verona: Fede & Cultura, 2017.

Fürer, Ivo. "Cardinal Hume's Influence in Europe." In *Basil Hume: Ten Years On.* Edited by William Charles. London: Burns and Oates, 2009.

Garzonio, Marco. *Il Profeta: Vita di Carlo Maria Martini.* Milan: Mondadori, 2012.

Goldberg, Leah. *Russian Literature in the Nineteenth Century.* Israel: Magnes Press, 1976.

Guerriero, Elio. *Benedict XVI: His Life and Thought.* San Francisco: Ignatius Press, 2010.

Hebblethwaite, Peter. *The Next Pope.* San Francisco: Harper, 1995.

Himitian, Evangelina. *Francisco: El Papa de la Gente.* Aguilar, 2013.

Ivereigh, Austen. *The Great Reformer: Francis and the Making of a Radical Pope.* New York: Henry Holt & Co., 2014.

Ivereigh, Austen. *Wounded Shepherd: Pope Francis and His Struggle to Convert the Catholic Church.* New York: Henry Holt, 2019.

Kaiser, Robert Blair. *A Church in Search of Itself: Benedict XVI and the Battle for the Future.* New York: Vintage, 2006.

Kasper, Walter. *Essential Spiritual Writings.* Edited by Robert A. Krieg and Patricia C. Bellm. Maryknoll, NY: Orbis, 2016.

Kasper, Walter. *Martin Luther: An Ecumenical Perspective.* Translated by William Madges. New York: Paulist Press, 2016.

Kasper, Walter. *Pope Francis' Revolution of Tenderness and Love.* Translated by William Madges. New York: Paulist Press, 2015.

Kasper, Walter. *The Catholic Church: Nature, Reality, and Mission.* London: Bloomsbury, 2015.

Kasper, Walter. *The Gospel of the Family.* Translated by William Madges. New York: Paulist Press, 2014.

Kengor, Paul. *The Devil and Karl Marx.* Gastonia, NC: TAN Books, 2020.

Küng, Hans. *Can We Save the Catholic Church?* London: William Collins, 2013.

Lawler, Philip. *Lost Shepherd: How Pope Francis Is Misleading His Flock.* Washington, DC: Regnery Gateway, 2018.

Lecomte, Bernard. *Secretos del Vaticano.* Buenos Aires: El Ateneo, 2014.

Le Gendre, Olivier. *Confession d'un Cardinal.* Paris: JC Lattès, 2007.

Le Gendre, Olivier. *L'Espérance du Cardinal.* Paris: JC Lattès, 2011.

Maradiaga, Óscar Rodríguez. *Only the Gospel Is Revolutionary: The Church in the Reform of Pope Francis.* Translated by Demetrio Yocum. Collegeville, MN: Liturgical Press, 2018.

Martini, Carlo Maria. "A Boon to Us All." In *Basil Hume: By His*

Friends. Edited by Carolyn Butler. London: Harper Collins, 1999.

Martini, Carlo Maria. *Perseverance in Trials: Reflections on Job.* United States: Liturgical Press, 1992.

Martini, Carlo Maria. *Qualcosa di Cosi Personale: Meditazioni sulla Preghiera.* Milan: Mondadori, 2009.

Martini, Carlo Maria and Georg Sporschill. *Night Conversations with Cardinal Martini.* Translated by Lorna Henry. New York: Paulist Press, 2012.

Mettepenningen, Jürgen and Karim Schelkens. *Godfried Danneels: Biographie.* Antwerpen: Uitgeverij Polis, 2015.

Millenari, The. *Shroud of Secrecy: The Story of Corruption Within the Vatican.* Translated by Ian Martin. Toronto: Key Porter Books, 2000.

Modena, Damiano. *Carlo Maria Martini: Il Silenzio della Parola.* Milan: San Paolo, 2013.

Murphy-O'Connor, Cormac. *An English Spring: Memoirs.* London: Bloomsbury, 2015.

Murphy-O'Connor, Cormac. *From the Vision of Pope John XXIII to the Era of Pope Francis.* Redemptorist, 2017.

Neumayr, George. *The Political Pope: How Pope Francis Is Delighting the Liberal Left and Abandoning Conservatives.* New York: Center Street, 2017.

O'Connell, Gerard. *The Election of Pope Francis: An Inside Account of the Conclave that Changed History.* Maryknoll, NY: Orbis, 2019.

Pentin, Edward. *The Rigging of a Vatican Synod: An Investigation into Alleged Manipulation at the Extraordinary Synod on the Family.* San Francisco: Ignatius Press, 2015.

Piqué, Elisabetta. *Pope Francis: Life and Revolution: A Biography of Jorge Bergoglio.* Chicago: Loyola Press, 2014.

Politi, Marco. *Joseph Ratzinger: Crisi di un Papato.* Rome: Laterza, 2015.

Politi, Marco. *Pope Francis Among the Wolves: The Inside Story of a Revolution.* New York: Columbia University Press, 2014.

Pope Francis. *God Is Young.* New York: Random House, 2018.

Rahner, Karl. *The Shape of the Church to Come.* London: S.P.C.K., 1974.

Ratzinger, Joseph. *Milestones: Memoirs.* San Francisco: Ignatius Press, 1998.

Ratzinger, Joseph. *The Ratzinger Report: An Exclusive Interview on the State of the Church.* San Francisco: Ignatius Press, 1985.

Ratzinger, Joseph and Peter Seewald. *Salt of the Earth: The Church at the End of the Millennium.* San Francisco: Ignatius Press, 2017.

Scalfari, Eugenio. *Il Dio Unico e la Società Moderna: Incontri con Papa Francesco e il Cardinale Carlo Maria Martini.* Torino: Einaudi, 2019.

Seewald, Peter. *Benedict XVI: A Life (Vol. 1).* Translated by Dinah Livingstone. London: Bloomsbury, 2020.

Seewald, Peter. *Benedict XVI: An Intimate Portrait.* Translated by Henry Taylor and Anne Englund Nash. San Francisco: Ignatius, 2008.

Socci, Antonio. *Non è Francesco. La Chiesa Nella Grande Tempesta.* Milan: Mondadori, 2015.

Spadaro, Antonio and Carlos María Galli. *For a Missionary Reform of the Church: The La Civiltà Cattolica Seminar.*

Mahwah, NJ: Paulist Press, 2017.

Tornielli, Andrea. *Carlo Maria Martini: El Profeta del Diálogo.* Santander: Sal Terrae, 2013.

Tosatti, Marco. *Neovatican Gallery.* Italy: Edizioni Radio Spada, 2021.

Vallely, Paul. *Pope Francis: The Struggle for the Soul of Catholicism.* London: Bloomsbury, 2015.

Vallely, Paul. *Pope Francis: Untying the Knots.* London: Bloomsbury, 2015.

Valli, Aldo Maria. *Benedetto XVI: Il Pontificato Interrotto.* Milan: Mondadori, 2013.

Valli, Aldo Maria. *Storia di un Uomo: Ritratto di Carlo Maria Martini.* Milan: Ancora, 2011.

Vorgrimler, Herbert. *Understanding Karl Rahner: An Introduction to His Life and Thought.* New York: Crossroad, 1986.

Wiltgen, Ralph. *The Inside Story of Vatican II: A Firsthand Account of the Council's Inner Workings.* Charlotte, NC: TAN Books, 2014.